The Experiences of Uncle Jack

Being a Biography of Rev. Andrew Jackson Newgent

W. Ed. Snyder

Alpha Editions

This edition published in 2021

ISBN : 9789355340153

Design and Setting By
Alpha Editions
www.alphaedis.com
Email - info@alphaedis.com

Contents

PREFACE

That which requires an apology should be left undone. Hence, the author of this humble work offers no apology in sending it forth. If it finds favor in the sight of those into whose hands it may fall, he will appreciate it. If not, it is confidently assumed that the world will pursue its wonted course, and no one will be the worse, if not the wiser.

No special literary excellence is claimed for it. It is a feeble, though honest, attempt to preserve from the cold, merciless realm of oblivion a life story that is well worth preserving—the life story of one for whom I have come to have the profoundest reverence and affection. My only regret is that it has not been done better.

Its chief value consists in the fact that it reveals the fundamental elements of true character and true success. The life of "Uncle Jack" Newgent is a conspicuous illustration of the fact that each individual is the architect of his own fate or fortune, that the conditions of success are internal and not external. This has been his life philosophy and has been abundantly vindicated by his life record. His right to a proper regard among his fellows rests upon his sterling qualities of manhood, devotion to a great purpose, and personal achievements that have added to the sum total of the world's weal and worth. He belongs to a worthy line of foundation builders whose work underlies the great superstructures of both church and state of the present day.

Hence, two purposes have been kept in view in the writing of this sketch— to acknowledge, if not to pay, a debt of honor and gratitude the Church owes to a worthy man; and by giving special attention to those personal qualities that make for success always and everywhere, and which were so strikingly exemplified in his character, to preserve the lessons of his life to the present and future generations in the hope that they may thus contribute to the further progress of righteousness. If in this unpretentious little volume these purposes are in any degree fulfilled, I shall be abundantly satisfied.

W. E. SNYDER.

INTRODUCTION

The pleasing task of writing an introduction to the life of my noble friend, Rev. A. J. Newgent, has fallen upon me. The intimate association which I have had with him for many years gives me a peculiar pleasure in seeing the record of his splendid life placed before the Church.

Biography is one of the most important departments of literature, and Mr. Newgent is eminently worthy of the permanent place in history which this volume accords him. I feel that fitting tributes in historic sketches should not only be paid the men of God who have planted the Church in this nation, but posterity should come and say over their graves, as Pericles did over the bodies of his fallen fellow soldiers: "You are like the divinities above us: you are known only by the benefits you have conferred." It is of such a man, though still living among us, that Dr. W. E. Snyder gives the accurately drawn portraiture in the chapters of this well-written biography. The work has been prepared with good judgment and much skill. The incidents of his life are given in sufficient detail, and make the volume exceedingly interesting and instructive. Such a publication is of great value, not only to those who enter the ministry, but to the whole Church, and especially to the young. To study the career of one, who, by fortitude and zeal, has carved his way from humble surroundings to a high place of honor among his fellow-men—passing through varied and striking vicissitudes in the struggle—can but inspire and ennoble other lives.

Entering the ministry before our pioneer style of life had passed away in the west, Mr. Newgent adapted himself to the humblest conditions of society. The fields of labor which he occupied in those early years of his pastorate were sufficient to remind him of the privation and hardships of those who had preceded him; but no condition was humble enough or severe enough to deter him from the work to which his young life had been consecrated. He could lodge in the loft of the lowliest cabin and subsist upon the cheapest fare. In quest of souls he thought little of anything else. Living among the people, a very small salary would suffice for him. He knew what it was to live on a moiety of one hundred dollars and less. There have been no dangers or hardships, no toils or privations, no suffering or sorrow sufficient to daunt his heroic spirit. Fortunately, Mr. Newgent is so constructed as to see the bright side of every difficulty, and his inimitable humor has made his family and friends laugh in the darkest hours of his ministerial life.

Unflinching loyalty to the Church has ever marked the career of Mr. Newgent. Though he has been peculiarly free from sectarian prejudices or bitterness, his attachment to his own people has been conscientious and unwavering. All his energies have been devoted to the advancement of the

Church of his choice. He has stood for the defense of its doctrines and polity, and those who have drawn him into debate over any feature of our system have not challenged him a second time. In the earlier days of his ministry he was many times called in debate with the strongest men of other denominations, and has proved himself equal to any antagonist who has met him in discussion. Many have gone down before his unanswerable arguments, and not a few have been driven from the contest because they could not stand before the torrent of his eloquence and the indescribable power of his wit. In all his ministerial work these qualities have often been of great advantage to him. Few men could possess such wit and eccentricities as Mr. Newgent commands, and use them to advantage without some objection by the people. But like all his other gifts, these peculiar qualities have been consecrated to the service of doing good, and in their use he has maintained his ministerial consecration and influence with never a breath of suspicion cast upon his good name.

It is gratifying to his many friends that Mr. Newgent, though retired from the active work of the ministry, is still in possession of all his mental powers, and no doubt will live to read his own biography. Few men have been so fortunate. To have spent his long and useful life in the most interesting period of the history of the Church, and then remain to read the part he has played in the making of that history, is a privilege that most of Christ's embassadors have never enjoyed. Back when the Publishing House was struggling for existence, he loyally supported the little plant, and never failed to circulate our books and push our periodicals in every charge he has filled. When our institutions of learning were in their infancy, and much opposition was brought against education, he was a friend of the schools, and again and again has gone into the field to raise money for their support. He has seen the great benevolent boards of the Church and nearly all our connectional institutions come up from the smallest beginnings, and has never failed to espouse the cause of these important agencies for the promotion of Christ's kingdom. Even the conference in which he began his ministry has grown in his day from a handful to a host, and no man has watched its growth with deeper pride or more anxious concern than himself.

I could write much more in the line of these thoughts, but the chapters of this volume will give in clear light the characteristics which can only be hinted at in the limits of an introduction. The skilled pen of the biographer will bring out in forceful and charming manner the noble traits of the gifted brother whose career he has studied with great care and painstaking interest. Let the book have a wide circulation, let the youth read its inspiring sentiments, and the horizon of their thoughts will be enlarged and the desire to be loyal to God and to every good work will be stimulated and strengthened.

T. C. CARTER.

November 27, 1911.

Chapter One.

Ancestry—Picture of Pioneer Life—Imprisonment and Release of Pompey Smash—Little Jack's Short Cut in the Study of Astronomy—The Fate of his First Pair of Breeches.

Once upon a time, so long ago that the chronology of it has become hidden in the mists of historical uncertainties, a man with his family emigrated from the hill section of northern Ireland to the vicinity of Dublin. What his real name was also belongs to the realm of the unknown, but among the unsophisticated rural inhabitants with whom he had cast his lot he was characterized simply as the "new gentleman." In course of time, the somewhat cumbersome title became abbreviated to "new gent," the original appellation finally passing from common usage entirely. That this new gentleman was a person of some force of character may be inferred from the distinction he seems to have achieved among his new neighbors and the fact that the name has been honored by men of rank and eminence among his descendants, a conspicuous example being Lord Robert Newgent (or Nugent), the celebrated Irish scholar and statesman.

Among the later descendants were three brothers who decided to cast their fortunes with the land of dreams and fancies across the Atlantic. Their names were Edward, William, and Thomas Newgent. On reaching America Edward directed his course toward the sunny South, William remained somewhere in the East, while Thomas struck out toward the vast region of unbroken forests on the western slopes of the Alleghenies. His pilgrimage terminated somewhere in the bounds of Kentucky. He secured a tract of land near Cincinnati, and in process of time met, wooed, and won a wealthy daughter of Virginia. He was contemporary with the Boones in reclaiming this great region of possibilities for civilization; helped to survey the State; taught school on both sides of the Ohio River, winning for himself the title of "Irish Schoolmaster," which, in this case, carried with it no small degree of distinction. He was a soldier in three wars, that of the Revolution, of 1812, and the Blackhawk War, for which services he received a pension from the Government. He professed religion at the ripe age of eighty, and was spared to redeem in part his long neglected opportunities by spending almost a quarter of a century in active Christian service, his long and eventful life closing, according to an uncertain tradition, in the 103d year of his age. He was the father of Charles Newgent, who was the father of Andrew Jackson Newgent, the hero of this simple narrative.

In Charles Newgent the elements of character peculiar to his race were exceptionally strong. A most marked propensity was his fondness for a joke. He would take more interest in concocting some new trick to be played on a neighbor or in devising a scheme for merrymaking than in a critical study of the Sermon on the Mount, or in solving an intricate theological problem. But while the religious faculty remained somewhat dormant, he was warm-hearted and generous, a good neighbor and citizen, according to the simple requirements of the times. In educational attainments he was far above the average. He was a prominent figure in local political circles, being a Jeffersonian Democrat of a rather emphatic type. His ever ready wit and fluency of speech made him a master on the stump and a formidable antagonist in political debates. The ability to give a humorous turn to any remark or incident served him well upon such occasions. His peculiar temperament gave him special aptitude as an auctioneer, in which capacity he had no superior. People would attend his sales as much to be entertained by his witticisms as for the bargains he might have to offer, and those who came to laugh often remained to settle a bill for something they had no thought of purchasing.

At the age of nineteen, in the year 1825, he was married to Mary Pugh, of Shelby County, Kentucky, his native county. Her parents had come from Scotland and were substantial citizens.

Soon after their marriage they moved to Parke County, Indiana, and settled on a tract of land which the wife had received as a dower from her father.

Pioneer life in Indiana need not here be enlarged upon. A solitary dwelling in the interminable and trackless forest; the building consisting of a single room built of unhewn logs, roofed with hand-split clapboards; the chimney covering one entire end of the building; the rough doors swung on wooden hinges; the small windows with greased paper or the tanned skins of animals through which a bit of daylight finds its way with difficulty; the huge fireplace used for both cooking and heating purposes; the few pieces of hand-made furniture—these were some of the outward aspects of domestic life out on the ragged edge of civilization. The cabin of the Newgents was typical of those of their neighbors, the nearest of whom lived some fifteen miles distant. The larger wild animals were frequent visitors and the war whoop of the Indian had scarcely died away.

After a brief residence at this place they moved to Sullivan County. Here, on Saturday, September 15, 1838, the subject of this sketch was born. He was the youngest of seven sons. Subsequently the family circle was enlarged by the addition of two daughters. The father's political bias was again asserted in the name, Andrew Jackson, assigned to this youngest son, after the great hero of early Democracy. The name often has given occasion for humorous touches by the owner, especially in referring to his early life. By the neighbors and older members of the family, he says, he was dubbed General Andrew Jackson. Later the military title was dropped and he became plain Andrew Jackson, and by successive stages the name was further abbreviated until the boy was doomed to answer to the simple cognomen of "Jack." Whether this was a process of evolution or of degeneration, he was destined to win for himself a title that would stand for real worth and attainment; that would represent the love of little children, as well as the esteem of men and women, when the affectionate appellation of "Uncle Jack" would become a household term in multitudes of homes.

Perhaps it is to the Scotch blood of his mother that he owes the more solid elements of his character. The Scotch character stands for thrift, energy, and integrity, so that wherever the hardy Scotchman goes he carries with him the best elements of citizenship. These combined with the quick wit and genial temperament of the sons of Erin produced in our subject a personality rich in depth and resourcefulness.

The emigration instinct, always strong in the pioneer, again became active, and the family set out for a new destination. This time it was Paw Paw Bend in Knox County, Indiana, so named because of its location in a bend of White River, and the prolific growth of paw paw trees for which the fertile lands were especially adapted. Our subject was then about eighteen months old. Here he spent the years of early childhood. Some incidents numbered among his earliest recollections and which serve to illustrate the home life and social conditions in which these years were passed, will not be out of place in this connection.

During this period religious services were practically unknown in Paw Paw Bend. The chief diversions were such social functions as shooting matches, wood choppings, log rollings, husking bees, and dances. The spelling bee was still of too intellectual a character to win popularity. At all such gatherings the familiar demijohn of corn whiskey was considered an indispensable adjunct.

Hence, the announcement of a preaching service to be held at the Newgent home on a following Sunday morning was hailed throughout the settlement as a new thing under the sun. Of course everybody would go. The preacher was to be Rev. Nathan Hinkle, a Methodist itinerant. It was out of no particular religious scruples that the host, Charles Newgent, volunteered to entertain the assemblage on this occasion, yet he had no aversion to preachers or churches, and in common with his neighbors, he was always ready to encourage anything that would break the monotony and afford social diversion.

It so happened that on Saturday evening before this memorable day, Pompey Smash, a negro fiddler, was passing through the neighborhood and asked to stay over night at Mr. Newgent's. He was informed by the head of the house that he would be furnished lodging on condition that he dispense music for a family dance. The terms were accepted and there was a sound of revelry by night as the little company beat time on the puncheon floor to the droll tunes of their musical guest.

Early next morning the congregation began to assemble for worship. The presence of the fiddler led to the suggestion that the time spent in waiting for the arrival of the preacher be used to the best possible advantage. Accordingly the Ethiopian turned his fiddle—for it was before the violin was invented; the familiar demijohn was set in a conspicuous place, and the gentlemen chose their partners. Lest the preacher's sudden arrival in the midst of such hilarious scenes be the occasion of a shock or an offense to his ecclesiastical dignity, a member of the party was dispatched to do picket service. The watchman, having imbibed too freely of the contents of the jug, fell asleep at his post. The dance had gone on merrily for some time in its rapturous excitement; the preacher and church service were utterly forgotten. When, lo! the alarm was sounded. The faithless watchman had allowed the company to be taken by surprise. The approach of the reverend was discovered in the nick of time; the dance came to an abrupt stop. To prevent the minister from "smelling a rat," a puncheon was removed hastily from the floor, and the fiddler, the fiddle, and the whiskey jug were thrust unceremoniously through the opening into the cellar excavation below. And the people put on their Sunday faces for church.

After the services a part of the congregation, including the shepherd of the flock, remained for dinner. This necessarily prolonged the imprisonment of the negro, but when it is recalled that the whiskey jug was a prison companion, we may surmise that the hours were not so "tedious and tasteless" as otherwise they might have been. The solemnities of the day came to an end with the departure of the minister; the prison was then opened and the prisoner released. An "after service" followed, which, it may be conjectured, was more in harmony with the tastes of the congregation.

While unlimited resources lay at the very doors of these pioneer cabins, the backwoodsmen lacked the facilities for developing them. Their tastes were not so exacting as in later days, and beyond the sheer necessities and comforts of the household, ambition did not spur them on. While ordinarily the family dined on homely fare, the industrious housewife often became so proficient in the culinary art as to be able to concoct most tempting dishes with the raw products that nature placed in easy reach. The sap of the maple tree, wild grapes, paw paws, and persimmons, as well as the products of garden, orchard, and field were utilized in providing for their physical wants.

Persimmons ripened with the early frosts, and when put up in maple syrup, became a staple and most delicious article of diet. By the addition of the proper quantity of whiskey, the standard remedy for most of the ills the flesh is heir to, the mixture afforded in addition to its other virtues, a sure cure for ague, commonly called "ager." This led to an episode in which little Jack and three older brothers were the leading figures, and which he facetiously labeled "a short cut in the study of astronomy."

The children were left alone one afternoon. The oldest of the quartet was familiar with the process of preparing the common ague antidote. The necessary ingredients were, as usual, within easy reach. So he proceeded to administer the remedy to his younger brothers on the principle that "if a little did good, more would do better." The bearing of this procedure upon the science of astronomy becomes apparent when we remember that among the unschooled of that day it was a mooted question as to whether or not the world is round and revolves upon its axis, as the geographies teach. Jack declared that after taking a few doses it was painfully evident to him that the world did turn round and turned at such a rapid rate that he found it difficult to keep from falling off. When the mother returned she found the three younger boys lying on the floor unconscious, and the author of the mischief sitting astride a joist overhead the unceiled room in a hilarious condition. By the free use of sweet milk the younger boys were restored to consciousness, but a special treatment was reserved for the one who led them into temptation. However, Jack found this short course in astronomy sufficient for all practical purposes, and he has never had the occasion or inclination to extend it.

His early years were as happy and free from care amid these primitive surroundings, as childhood life could well be, even in what might be considered more favorable circumstances. Life was simple in the extreme, even crude, but it was the best he knew. There was nothing in the lives of his associates calculated to excite envy or cause discontent with his own lot. But in this connection one incident stands out in bold relief to mar the picture of boyish contentment.

A single garment of homespun, or "tow linen," was all that was considered necessary in the way of clothing under ordinary circumstances for a boy of that age. It marked a new era in his life when the loose garment which covered the anatomy down to the knees was supplemented by a pair of breeches of the same material. Upon one occasion as Jack stood watching his mother as she was measuring the material for the older boys' winter suits, he heard her remark that there would probably be enough scraps left over to make him a pair of breeches. With emotions alternating between hope and fear, he waited impatiently for the outcome. His joy was unbounded when he found that his hopes were to be realized. His mother laid him on the floor and thus marked the pattern. It was seen that the closest economy had to be used to make the goods hold out; so instead of the regulation number of two suspenders which were one piece with the breeches, the material would only warrant the making of one. By extending it from one side on the back diagonally across the shoulder, making connection on the opposite side in front, the new habiliment maintained its balance and no special inconvenience was suffered.

But alas! his rejoicing was soon to be turned into mourning. A few days later, clad in his new outfit, he went with his brothers to the woods to gather pecans. It was a warm autumn afternoon, and in climbing and clubbing the trees and picking up the nuts, the boys found it convenient to cast off unnecessary articles of clothing. As Jack had scarcely become accustomed to more than one garment, he could easily dispense with the breeches for the time. Accordingly they were removed and hung on a bush near by, and for a time forgotten in the fascination of nut hunting. When the party was ready to start home with the fruits of their toil, he was alarmed to find that his cherished breeches had disappeared. The boys searched diligently but found them not. When about ready to give up in despair, they chanced to observe, a short distance away, a mellow-eyed, crinkly-horned, brindle cow making a meal off the lad's wearing apparel, or perhaps using it for dessert, as though it were a dainty morsel. And the last Jack saw of his first pair of breeches was the lone suspender dangling from the innocent old brindle's mouth, the major part of them having been engulfed in her capacious maw. And to the sorrow of his heart, his wardrobe for another year was limited to the single piece of homespun.

CHAPTER TWO.

The Tragic Death of the Father—Removal to Parke County—School Days—Conversion—Change of Church Relationship—A Remarkable Providence.

Thus far our narrative has covered the childhood of our subject up to the ninth year of his age. At this juncture occurred an event that cast the first real shadow over his youthful pathway. It was the death of his father, the tragic nature of which and the subsequent effect it was to have upon his career, made the shadow all the deeper and more significant. Charles Newgent went with a company consisting of sixty adventurous spirits, upon an expedition to the West, the real object of which seems to be somewhat indefinite. The restless and venturesome spirit of the pioneer, a curious desire to penetrate the mysteries of the great western world, the dream of untold treasures that nature had in store for those who dared to conquer the dragons that guarded them—all may have figured in this ill-fated enterprise. However that may have been, while crossing the western plains the company was attacked and massacred by a band of hostile Indians. As in the calamities that befell Job's household, one of the number was left to tell the story. This one was supposed by the savages to have shared the fate of all the rest, being left on the field for dead; but it so happened that in his case the weapon of death did not do complete work. He was picked up the next day by a party of hunters to whom he was able to give a vague account of the preceding day's terrible tragedy.

After the father's death, the mother with her nine children moved back to their former home in Parke County. Life then took on a sterner aspect for the boy. His tender hands must perform their part in the maintenance of the family. Accordingly he hired out to Mr. Jesse Maddox, a neighboring farmer. His wages the first year were to be a pair of shoes, ten bushels of corn, and the privilege of attending the district school. The market price of corn was ten cents per bushel. Even at this modest stipend he admits that he made money, "though not very much." While in after years of fruitful labors in the ministry he often remarked that the question that most perplexed him was how to earn what he received, it is not probable that the question at this time had assumed very serious proportions.

The most important stipulation in the contract was the privilege of attending school. But even this is subject to shrinkage when we recall that the school system of Indiana was then in its first stage of development. It afforded no royal path to learning, and the common thoroughfare was neither smooth nor flowery. We would scarcely expect to find in the schoolroom comforts that the home itself was a stranger to. Strikingly suggestive of the interior aspect of those primitive seats of learning are the lines from Whittier's "In School Days":

"Within, the master's desk is seen,

Deep scarred by raps official;

The battered seats, the warping floor,

The jack knife's carved initial.

"The charcoal frescoes on the wall,

The door's worn sill betraying

The feet that creeping late to school,

Went storming out to playing."

To fit the particular building in which our subject first tasted the fruit of the tree of knowledge, the picture needs but slight modification. If anything, it should be made even more simple and primitive. The "battered" seats were made of puncheon. Since this word is passing from common usage, it may be well to explain that puncheon is made by splitting a small log in two equal parts. The split edges are then trimmed down, and the pieces thus treated served as a rough substitute for sawed lumber. To make them into seats, two holes were bored near each end in the unhewn side. These being at proper angles, wooden pins were inserted into them for legs. The rude seat was then ready for service. It is not to be taken for granted that these seats were always made perfectly smooth. What was lacking to smooth them down by the workmen was expected to be completed by the pupils. They finished the task, but often it was a long and painful process, with many a protest from a new gown of homespun or a pair of "tow-linen," home-grown breeches. Thus, with no rest for the arms or the back, with one side scorched by the heat from the great fireplace and the other chilled by the winter winds creeping through cracks in floor and walls and roof, the children wore away the dreary hours. The floor, being composed of this same puncheon, did not easily warp. The recess recreation consisted mainly in carrying fuel from the surrounding forest to feed the every-hungry fireplace.

Whatever dignity the schoolmaster may have possessed in the eyes of his pupils, certain it is he was not the original of Goldsmith's creation in the "Deserted Village," of whom the wonder was "that one small head could carry all he knew." Beyond the traditional essentials of scholarship, consisting of reading, writing, and ciphering, with a specially intimate acquaintance with the spelling book, he did not pretend to lead. His chief business was to govern the school. He proved his divine right to his throne in the schoolroom by his ability to handle the most obstreperous cases the district could produce. The scholars were on hand as a challenge to his generalship. The hero of the school was the one who held out longest against his despotic authority. To lick the teacher was the height of his ambition. This realized, his place in the local hall of fame was secure. According to the philosophy of the times "lickin' and larnin'" went hand in hand, lickin' being essential, while larnin' was incidental.

The school house was three miles from the Maddox home. The school was maintained on the basis that "whosoever will may come." There was no penalty for tardiness or absence, but as young Newgent possessed a real thirst for knowledge and was in the habit of making the most of whatever he undertook, his attendance was more regular than the average. However, the sum total of his schooling was limited to three terms of about three months each, an aggregate of nine months. Meager as were his school advantages, they were well improved and furnished a foundation for self-culture upon which he built as only a genius can. He learned to read in less than four weeks, and his progress was correspondingly rapid throughout. His real school was not bounded by the walls of the log school house; it was rather the great school of life with its harsh discipline and inexhaustible curriculum; and in this he grew to be the peer of the ripest products of educational institutions. "Opportunities," he says, in his characteristic way, "the woods has always been full of opportunities. I had splendid opportunities when I was a boy, and so did my companions; but many of them, like some young folks now, failed to see them." He saw what many fail to see, that opportunities are not so much in our environment as in ourselves, and that success is not determined by outward circumstances, but by one's own will and energy.

A habit early formed was that of turning everything to account in the pursuit of knowledge. Mrs. Newgent, anxious to encourage her children's propensities for study, furnished the home with such reading matter as her means would permit. Though the family were separated most of the time, they came together at frequent intervals. On these occasions the time was well spent in reading and in discussing current topics. Whatever was read became the subject of conversation. These conversations often took the form of argument, in which the various sides of a subject were presented and zealously defended. Thus, he early displayed and developed an aptitude for argumentative discussion, which made him a master in debate, and is a strong element in all his public discourses.

His conversion occurred when he was about ten years old, while still in the service of Mr. Maddox, a benefit which was not considered in the contract with his employer. This took place during a gracious revival at the Canaan Methodist church, of which his employer was a member and was serving at the time as class leader and janitor. The meeting had been in progress for a number of days; many had found the Savior, and the community was deeply stirred. He had been sent to open the church and build the fire for the evening service. While going quietly about his duties, all alone, the impression came to him quite vividly that he ought to be a Christian, and he resolved to go to the "mourner's bench" that night. He was never long in making up his mind, and when a decision was once made, it was as a law of the Medes and Persians. So he went to the altar that night and each succeeding night for more than a week. One evening as he was listening to the sermon, conviction became so intense that in his extremity he left the house. Though it was a cold night and the ground was covered with snow, he stole out in the woods. Kneeling in the snow, this youthful Jacob wrestled with God in prayer. How long he tarried, he could not tell, but faith triumphed, and the next he knew the woods were resounding with his shouts of victory. Rushing into the church while the preacher was yet talking, he put an end to the sermon by his shouting and praising God. The congregation was electrified. Soon the demonstration became general, and for a time pandemonium held sway; but it was of a sort in which there were both method and meaning, for its source was from above.

Like God's servant of old, he could say, "My heart is fixed." He joined the church and from that time never missed an opportunity to pray and testify in public or private. At that time children did not receive much attention from the church. Churches were strong on saving souls from damnation, but the idea of saving the entire life for service had not taken deep root. As a result of the revival there was a large class of "probationers." When the period of probation had expired, according to the church law, and they were to be admitted into full membership, his name was not on the list. He was not considered a member; at least that was his version of it, and the only logical conclusion the case would warrant. It was a sore disappointment, but of too delicate a nature to mention to his elders. So he kept his feelings to himself.

Thus matters stood for little more than a year, when he learned that there was to be a quarterly meeting at the Otterbein United Brethren Church a few miles away. This church belonged to the Rockville Circuit of the Wabash Conference. Rev. William Sherrill was the pastor. The presiding elder, who was to hold the quarterly conference, was Rev. Samuel Zuck. Both were strong and good men. Jack had never attended a United Brethren service. What knowledge he had of the Church was gained through conversations overheard in the Maddox home. Ministers being frequently entertained there, conversation at such times naturally took to religious channels. As this was an age when churches did not entertain the most fraternal feelings toward one another, these conversations were not calculated, as a rule, to produce a favorable opinion of a rival denomination. His interest in churches and religion was genuine, born of a desire to know the truth. Hence, is was not mere curiosity that led him to obtain his employer's permission to spend Saturday and Sunday with a neighbor in the Otterbein community so that he might attend the services of the quarterly meeting.

The Church proved to be his affinity. Whatever misgivings he had, vanished one by one. The general atmosphere of the first service harmonized with his temperament. There was spirit in the singing. His heart burned within him as he listened to the eloquent sermon by the presiding elder; and when the pastor followed, as the custom was, with a warm exhortation, he was enraptured. He resolved to join the Church. As usual, the decision was made without much preliminary. He knew where he stood, and stood there with both feet. When he returned, his employer, as well as his own folks, was thunderstruck to learn that he had become a full-fledged United Brethren. Having put his hand to the plow, he never turned back. "I have been so busy," is a common saying with him, "that I have never had time to backslide."

It should be said in justice to the church where he first joined, that his name had been entered upon the book, but by mistake it was placed in the list with the full members. This accounts for his not being received with the probationers, to which class he belonged, and led to the conclusion that he was not considered a member. Thus an apparently insignificant thing may prove to be a matter of vital importance.

As a boy he possessed pronounced convictions and a keen sense of religious obligation. This is demonstrated by an incident which occurred while he was in the employ of Mr. Jerry Rush, a short time after leaving the service of Mr. Maddox. Mr. Rush was a well-to-do farmer and stock dealer. Neither he nor his wife made any profession of religion, though their lives were regarded as exemplary and above question in other respects. Some of the men who worked on the farm, however, were of the baser sort. It seemed strange to young Newgent that a man of Mr. Rush's habits would surround himself with men who were utterly destitute of moral scruples or of the commonest decencies. To him their vulgarity and profanity were a source of constant annoyance. At one time as their coarse jests were grating on his sensitive ears, he was impressed with the idea that this uncouth crowd afforded him a field for missionary work. The impression was not long in taking definite shape. It came with the force of a challenge, a bugle call to duty, a call that he never failed to heed. His mind was made up that he would offer prayer with these men before they retired that evening if Mr. Rush would grant him the privilege.

It was a bold resolve, an ordeal from which a braver heart might well have shrunk. Let eloquent tongues proclaim the praise of those who face death at the cannon's mouth, or the inspired pen immortalize the hero, who, amid the applause of admiring multitudes, imperils his own life to save another; but who would not count it a worthy act to place a laurel wreath upon the brow of a fourteen-year-old lad who dared to face, not one Goliath, but a company of Goliaths, with the simple weapon of faith, and demand that they bow before their God while he offered a petition in behalf of their needy souls? Yet this resolute purpose was to undergo a severe test. The fiercest battles are fought in our own hearts. As the time drew near, he felt his courage slipping away. He stole out to the barn for a time of secret prayer, that he might be equal to the emergency. Feeling comforted and strengthened, he started to the house to execute his plan. On reaching the yard gate his courage seemed to take flight, and he could go no farther. He went back to the place of prayer. On the second venture he got as far as the door, when his strength again vanished. Not to be beaten, he went back to the barn to fight the battle to a finish. The third effort won the day. He hastened to the house, determined not to give the enemy a chance. The men were sitting about the fire. Without a word by way of preliminary, he stepped up to Mr. Rush and asked permission to kneel with them in prayer. The permission was granted, and a solemn hush came over the startled company as they listened while the boy, with trembling voice and stammering accents, poured out his soul to God. He then sought his bed with the consciousness that he had done his duty. A sweet peace filled his soul and he lay for hours in ecstacy of joy.

The next evening the family devotions were repeated. But on the third evening the prayer was forestalled by a preconcerted plan on the part of the men. As the time for prayer approached, one after another, they arose and stalked out of the room, and the victor in two hard-fought battles was left alone—defeated and dejected. His spirits dropped down to zero. The fiery dart had pierced him through and through. In agony of soul he sought his bed, but not to rest. Out of the depth of his troubled heart he called upon God for comfort. But the fury of the storm seemed only to increase. In his desperation he felt that something must be done. So, about the hour of midnight, he arose, dressed himself, and left the house to go—he knew not where. Through the remaining hours of the night he wandered, directing his course toward the West. Daylight came, the sun rose above the horizon and pursued its course toward the zenith, but his pilgrimage continued. At noon he found himself in the city of Terre Haute, then a mere village. Here he tarried for a time to seek employment. Failing in this, he resumed his westward journey. He asked for work at the various farm houses which he passed. While he found kind hearts who, touched by pity for the youthful pilgrim, gave him food and temporary shelter, he found no man to hire him until he reached Mattoon, Illinois, nearly a hundred miles from whence he started. Work at that season of the year was scarce, and his term of service at Mattoon was brief. At the end of three days his employer gave him his wages with the intelligence that his services were no longer needed.

He now decided to go back to Indiana. With his three days' wages in his pocket, with which he expected to pay for his transportation at least part of the way, he set out upon the return journey. Within the vicinity of Terre Haute he succeeded in finding steady employment and a congenial home.

There were two sides to this story, and some months after Jack was settled in his new home he learned the other side. It was glorious news to him. The sequel was that Mr. Rush was converted, joined the Baptist Church, and became a zealous leader in religious work. It came about in this way: When Mr. Rush found that Jack had disappeared and diligent effort failed to solve the mystery of his disappearance, a feeling of remorse over his unchristian conduct so possessed him that for days he was almost in a state of frenzy. Remorse took the form of spiritual conviction and genuine repentance which led to a glorious conversion.

On learning of the whereabouts of his young benefactor, Mr. Rush at once went to see him, and told him his side of the story. He confessed to Jack that he was a guilty party to the scheme the men had used to defeat him. The boy's awkward prayer together with their own antipathy for such pious exercises was a source of embarrassment to the men, and they agreed among themselves to use the method described to rid themselves of further annoyance. Little did Mr. Rush realize that those awkward prayers were to be the means of his salvation.

"God moves in a mysterious way,

His wonders to perform,

He plants his footsteps on the sea,

He rides upon the storm.

"Judge not the Lord with feeble sense,

But trust him for his grace,

Behind a frowning providence

He hides a smiling face."

CHAPTER THREE

Call to the Ministry—First Sermon—The Boy Preacher—Answering a Fool After his Folly—Turning a Camp Meeting Tide—Quieting a Skirmish—Takes a Wife.

Providence seemed to ordain that there should be one preacher in the Newgent family and that that one should be Jack. As has been observed, his religious zeal from the time of his conversion at the age of ten, was exceptional. Just when the first impression looking toward the ministry came to him he could scarcely tell, such impressions having been associated more or less with his religious experience from the beginning. By the time he was thirteen the conviction that he had a "divine call" to preach the gospel became clear and definite. And the conviction deepened with the passing of time. Of course, no one dreamed of the emotions that were stirring the boy's breast, and to him the ministry was so high and sacred a calling as to seem infinitely beyond his possibilities. Hence, he dared not express his feelings to even his most intimate friends, and so received no sympathy or encouragement from any human source. He went about his Father's business in his own way, rendering such service to the cause of his Master as a boy of his years was capable of. His zeal knew no abatement, and such diligence is sure to lead to recognition and reward.

The minister who first took a special interest in him was Rev. Ira Mater, an able preacher and a sympathetic discerner of the thoughts and intents of the heart. Between the man and the lad there sprang up a beautiful friendship, suggestive of that between Paul and Timothy. Rev. Mr. Mater frequently invited his young friend to accompany him to his appointments, and by way of stirring up the gift that was in this prospective Timothy, sometimes called upon him to open the service, to exhort after the sermon, or perform such other public ministrations as were convenient. Rev. Mr. Newgent has always gratefully acknowledged his indebtedness to this spiritual father.

This association with Rev. Mr. Mater was during his sixteenth and seventeenth years. He was small and rather delicate for one of his age. His entire youth was a continual conflict with disease, the entire category of which seemed to try their hand upon his slender frame. But while his body was frail, his mind was strong and alert. That his positive temperament and seeming disposition to never give up had somewhat to do in staving off the grim monster, death, is not at all unlikely.

His first regular discourse was preached at the Stedd School House near Fontanet, in Clay County, Indiana. The school house was used as a preaching point and weekly prayer meetings were maintained. He was a frequent attendant at these services, and one evening, on entering the house, he was met by the leader who said, "Jack, the people are expecting you to preach to-night." That he was to preach was simply a surmise, his association with Rev. Mr. Mater being the probable foundation of it. But some one surmised out loud and the rumor gained currency. Observing his surprise at this intelligence, the leader continued, "You had just as well begin here and now," in a manner that indicated that it was a foregone conclusion that preaching was to be his life business. And Jack preached. At any rate, if the effort could not be classed as preaching, it was a splendid substitute for it. He announced as a text, "If the righteous scarcely be saved, where shall the ungodly and the sinner appear?" The congregation was visibly affected by his fervor and earnestness, some of the more demonstrative ones giving vent to their feelings in shouts of praise. He was urged to preach the next night, and the meetings were continued for more than a week, being held at various private homes, Newgent preaching at each service. The divine seal was thus placed upon his ministry, and the meeting marked the beginning of a new epoch in his career.

A few weeks later the Rockville quarterly conference granted him a license to preach. The action was taken in his absence. J. P. White was the preacher in charge and Thomas M. Hamilton was the presiding elder. The action of the quarterly conference was almost a superfluous formality, as he was now so greatly in demand that he could not well avoid preaching.

The boy preacher was a popular character. To see a man on the *ante meridian* of life in the pulpit was at that time quite unusual. The popular prejudice was in favor of men who had spent the major part of their lives on the farm or in business, thus acquiring a competence that would enable them to proclaim that salvation is free without being embarrassed or embarrassing their congregations on the money question. Hence, a diminutive lad of seventeen, weighing only about eighty pounds, exercising the ministerial function was in itself sufficient to attract the multitudes. Wherever he preached he was greeted by immense audiences. By many he was regarded as a prodigy, though he could not be classed as such, prodigies seldom accomplishing more than to afford amusement for curious spectators. It is true, however, that he displayed qualities unusual for one of his years, though it must be admitted that the greater part of his power lay in his intense religious zeal and earnestness.

Some characteristic incidents in this part of his ministry will not only be of interest in themselves, but will at the same time serve to illustrate his unique individuality. He went on one occasion to fill an appointment at what was known as the Rough and Ready School House. The name was justified by the prevailing social conditions. Like Paul on Mars Hill, he found that at least some of the people were very religious, though their religious energy was not always directed to the best advantage. Not infrequently does it transpire that men will fight for their religion even when they are utterly averse to the practice of it, a fact which had a forcible illustration in this particular service. He preached with his usual energy. The house was crowded and the sermon seemed to be well received. There happened to be present a minister of what was designated as the Campbellite persuasion. Evidently the sermon did not coincide with his theological bias. He asked permission to say a few words as the speaker took his seat. The permission granted, he sallied forth with a tirade of abuse and denunciation of the young preacher and his theology in which his passion played a larger part than either his judgment or his conscience. When he finally ran down, Newgent arose in a calm manner and said, "Brother, with your way of applying Scripture, I can prove that Eve was the mother of a turkey buzzard." "Prove it, then," shouted back the irascible theologue. "Well, the Bible says that Eve was the mother of all living, and that includes turkey buzzards. Let us be dismissed," and calling the audience to their feet, he pronounced the benediction before his assailant had time to reply.

At another time, with his brother, John Newgent, he happened to drop in at a Methodist camp meeting in Sullivan County. They arrived just in time for the morning service. A number of ministers were seated on the platform, among them being Rev. Hayden Hayes, the presiding elder. Rev. Mr. Hayes had met Newgent on a former occasion, and as soon as he saw him enter the camp, rushed back and taking him by the arm, led him to the platform. Hayes was a strong, portly man, and the delicate lad was helpless in his grasp; thus he was led as a lamb to the slaughter, and was informed that he must preach. Though he vainly sought to be excused, yet he was equal to the emergency. He had proceeded about ten minutes with his discourse, when a man sitting a few feet in front of the platform was converted and began to shout. He continued, and four others in the congregation broke loose in like manner, all of them having been converted through the effect of the sermon, and the discourse disappeared in a whirlwind of praise that completely drowned the speaker's voice. Up to that time there had been no move in the meeting.

John Newgent was imbued with the old-school Baptist doctrine and had not sympathized with his brother's preaching propensities. After resuming their journey they rode for a time in silence. Finally the older brother said, "Jack, you know I have always opposed your preaching. But I want to say that I have no further objection to it; but," he added with quivering lips, "I want you to pray for me." The sermon had touched his heart.

Though urgent demands were made upon the boy preacher to stay and assist in the meeting, he was unable to do so, and heard nothing further from it until after he had returned from the war, when by chance he again passed through the vicinity. He stopped at the home of a Mrs. Mayfield, on whose farm the camp was located, to get his dinner and his horse fed. As he was taking his leave, having paid his bill, he chanced to observe the camp ground a short distance away. Up to that time he was not aware that he was in the immediate vicinity of it. He inquired of his hostess concerning the camp meetings. She told him that but one such meeting had been held, though the intention was to make it a permanent institution. The unsettled condition of times during the Rebellion prevented the plan from being carried out.

"How was that meeting?" Newgent asked, as one who had a peculiar interest in it.

"Oh, it was a grand success. There was a little Baptist preacher from near Lafayette happened in and preached one morning, and just set things on fire. From that time on the meetings were powerful."

"What was the fellow's name?" he asked, but she could not recall it.

"Was it Newgent?" She said that sounded like it.

"Well," he said, "I know him. He isn't considered much of a preacher up there where he lives, but," he added, "you are mistaken about his being a Baptist. He is a United Brethren."

She looked at him curiously for an instant and said, "I believe you are the fellow." And his smile told that she had guessed aright.

His money was returned at once, and she insisted that he stay and preach at the Methodist church near the camp ground that night, assuring him that he would have a good hearing as there had been much talk about the little preacher who had "set the camp meeting afire." This he was unable to do, but promised to return at a later date.

A short while after the camp meeting, he filled an appointment for his pastor, Rev. J. F. Moore, at the Leatherwood church, which was a part of the Rockville charge. The pulpit arrangement of this church was in strict harmony with the fashion of the times. It consisted of a sort of wall which shut the preacher in almost completely from the congregation, suggesting a military fortification. Newgent, being small of stature, could with difficulty peer over the top of the ramparts. He was led to believe, however, that the fortification was a necessary precaution, for his artillery had been turned loose but a short time when it was evident that there was a hearty response. Bang! Some sort of a missile struck the rampart just in front of him with a loud report. It was followed immediately by another, and the bombardment, continued until six discharges were fired. The preacher withdrew within the breastworks that small fraction of his anatomy that was exposed, and waited for hostilities to cease. The congregation was at once thrown into a state of confusion and excitement. When the preacher finally surveyed the situation after the heavy batteries were silenced, he saw that a hand-to-hand skirmish was on between two men in the rear of the room. One was making a desperate effort to get the other to the door and out of the house. With the help of the congregation, he succeeded in putting down the rebellion, and going back to his fortifications he finished the discourse and the service was concluded in fairly good order. The difficulty was only a side issue, the culmination of a grudge between a couple of natives. The missiles were not aimed at the preacher, but were fired from ambush through the open door; the man for whom they were intended happened to be sitting in range with the pulpit.

Rev. Mr. Moore resigned the Rockville charge during the year and Newgent was appointed to serve the unexpired term. This was his first experience in the pastorate. His brief term of service here was characterized by a revival of extraordinary results at Otterbein, his home church. Converts were numbered by the scores and the community was shaken by such a spiritual upheaval as it had never known.

REV. ANDREW JACKSON NEWGENT

When he traveled his first circuit.

Another adventure should be chronicled here. It has been said that there are but three real important events in a man's life, namely, his birth, his marriage, and his death. The second of this great trio in the life of our subject occurred during the period embraced in this chapter. It is a common saying with him that he does not believe in early marriages, hence, he deferred this important step until he was eighteen years old. And on the seventh of January, 1857, he took to himself a wife in the person of Miss Katharine Copeland. She proved to be a worthy and sympathetic companion, heroically assuming her part of the burdens and responsibilities that belong to the family of an itinerant preacher. That her lot was not an easy one may be readily assumed when we consider what the ministerial calling involved in that early day. Its peculiar hardships fell most heavily upon the wife, yet these she endured without protest. Brave in heart, gentle in temper, and in heartiest accord with her husband's interests, she proved to him a real helpmeet, and an inspiration to his loftiest endeavors.

CHAPTER FOUR.

Conference Membership—Brulitz Creek Ministry—The Modern Knight and his Steed—Abrupt Closing of Family Devotions by a Dog on the Preacher—An Original Marriage Ceremony—A Case of Mistaken Identity—A Banner Missionary Collection—Shawnee Prairie Pastorate—A Cold Day in April—The Redemption of Hell's Half Acre—Baiting for a Perverse Fish—An Experience in the Whiskey Business.

Rev. Mr. Newgent was received into the Upper Wabash Conference at Milford, Indiana, in the spring of 1859. Bishop David Edwards presided. The Conference had been formed the preceding year by a division of the Wabash Conference territory. As a matter of coincidence he was ordained four years later at the Conference in session at the same place with the same Bishop presiding. He was now in his twenty-first year, having been quite prominent in ministerial labors for about four years, and had a record for zeal, earnestness, and success in revival work that commended him favorably to the Conference.

He was appointed by this Conference to the Brulitz Creek Circuit, which gave him an unlimited field for the exercise of his zeal and talents. The circuit consisted of eighteen appointments, only two of which were at church-houses; the others were at school houses and in private homes. With little or no competition, the circuit-rider was monarch of all he surveyed, though in most cases when he received his appointment he found enough already surveyed to tax his time and energy to the limit. Preaching services were not confined to the Sabbath, but would fall upon any day of the week, and even then the intervals between appointments, except during the periodic "big meeting," were usually not less than five or six weeks.

The standard mode of travel was by horseback, and the circuit-rider, in addition to his other qualifications, needed to be efficient in horsemanship. This was scarcely necessary in Newgent's case, however. Not being able to own a horse at this time, he secured the loan of one from an accommodating neighbor. The horse was as accommodating as its owner. It was quite well "broke," having endured the rigors of some nineteen winters, and was experienced in the various departments of farm work. It had sowed and reaped—and eaten—its wild oats, and was absolutely reliable, at least to the limit of its physical endurance. At any rate the horse had many acknowledged good points, as a faithful portrait would have demonstrated. While it may not have been in its real element on dress parade, it served the more practical purpose of locomotion—to a somewhat limited extent.

As the rider weighed scarcely a hundred pounds, the horse had no cause to complain at his burden. And when it came to matters of appearance, the odds were not so unevenly balanced as might be supposed. The spare-built, smooth-faced youth, clad in his suit of homespun, which was made with a reckless disregard of the lines and proportions of his anatomy, might well have recalled the lines of Shakespeare:

"Would that he were fatter, but I fear him not;

Yet if my name were liable to fear,

I know of no one whom I would so much avoid."

Thus, mounted upon his trusty steed, armed with all the weapons of spiritual warfare, this modern knight errant of the saddle-bags rode forth valiantly to the scenes of the year's conflicts and triumphs. En-route to his first appointment, he found an opportunity to do some pastoral work which led to an episode, without mention of which these chronicles would be incomplete. Passing by the home of one of his prominent members, he stopped for a brief call. The house stood on the side of a hill, some distance from the road. A flight of steps led up to the front door. Ascending the steps, he rapped at the door and was kindly admitted by the good housewife. All went merry as a marriage bell and the time of his departure was at hand all too soon. He asked the privilege of bowing with the family in prayer before going, which was freely granted. The weather was warm and it was not thought necessary to close the door, though had it been done in this case, it would have prevented a bit of embarrassment and incidentally spoiled a good story. As all was so congenial within, the pastor anticipated no molestation from without, and so injudiciously knelt with his back to the open door.

As he warmed up to his devotions, he aroused from his slumbers a large Newfoundland dog, that had evidently not noticed the approach of the stranger, and up to that time was unaware of his presence. The aroused canine at once began an investigation, and when he saw what was going on, seemed much offended that he had not been consulted about the matter. He bounded up the steps into the room, and, seizing the preacher by the luxuriant growth of black hair that covered his dome of thought, affording an excellent hold for his teeth, he zealously set about the task of removing the supposed intruder from the premises. The preacher was taken unawares. Before he could assume a defensive attitude, he and the dog were rolling pell-mell, higgledy-piggledy over each other, down the steps, and landed in a confused heap on the ground. Devotions thus came to an abrupt close; the family came to the preacher's rescue. All formalities were dispensed with for the time. By the united efforts of the family, the dog and preacher were finally separated without either of them being seriously damaged, and the new pastor of Brulitz Creek Circuit went on his way to face new adversaries and new experiences.

Family Devotions Interrupted.

He reached the home of Mr. Jacob Wimsett, in Vermilion County, on Saturday evening as the sun was dropping below the horizon, and there put up for the night. This was in the vicinity of his Sunday morning appointment. It was an old-fashioned home even for that day; the home atmosphere was more hospitable than conventional. As the preacher himself was quite democratic in his temperament, no formalities were required. He noticed among the various members of the household a young man and a young woman who seemed as unobtrusive and as awkward as himself. No introductions being given, he took it for granted that they both were members of the family and so gave them no particular thought until he was ready to start to church the next morning. As he was about to take his leave, the young man approached him rather diffidently and requested him to wait a few minutes.

"Me an' the girl," he explained, pointing to the blushing lass on the opposite side of the room, "are a goin' to git married, an' we want you to say the words for us before you go."

"All right," said Newgent, in a manner that left the impression that he understood the situation all the while, "give me your license."

The document was produced and the twain took their place in front of the preacher, while the rest of the company looked on. Up to this time he had never served in that capacity and had not the slightest idea of a marriage ceremony. Examining the document in a seemingly critical manner for an instant as if to make sure that it conformed to all requirements, he looked gravely at the trembling young couple. "If you are agreed to live together," he said so rapidly as to render his words scarcely intelligible, "according to the marriage covenant, join your right hands." Scarcely had they time to heed the injunction when he continued, "In the name of God I pronounce you man and wife." And the twain were made one.

He then hastened to his morning appointment, reaching the church before the people began to gather. This was one of the two church-houses on the circuit, and was called Nicholls' Chapel. "Father" Nicholls, one of the wheel-horses of the church, and in whose honor it was named, was sweeping the floor and putting the house in order. His task completed, he went home to get ready for the morning service, without making the acquaintance of the young stranger. Ere long the people began to arrive. By the time Sunday school commenced the house was quite well filled. Newgent took his seat in the rear of the house and received no particular attention. He was not even invited to a place in a Sunday-school class. However, his presence *incognito* gave him a good opportunity for taking notes. He overheard frequent remarks concerning the new preacher. The people had heard nothing of him and were expressing doubts about his being in the neighborhood. And when Sunday school closed without his presence being made known, their doubts seemed to be confirmed.

Rev. William Jones, a retired preacher and a member of the local class, came in just as Sunday school was closing and at once made inquiry concerning the pastor.

"We haven't seen or heard anything of him," was the information he received from Father Nicholls.

"Why, there he is now," and Rev. Mr. Jones pointed to the diminutive lad near the door.

"That fellow?" Father Nicholls was dumfounded. "That fellow has been here all morning. I supposed he was some hired hand in the neighborhood that had just happened in."

Explanations and apologies were freely indulged in, the supposed hired hand entering heartily into the joke. He was introduced to the astonished congregation, and the service proceeded to their entire satisfaction and delight. Father Nicholls treated him kindly; he piloted him to the afternoon appointment, introducing him to all whom they chanced to meet, invariably accompanying the introduction with the story of the forenoon experience.

"If I had been out hunting for preachers," he would say, in telling the story, "I would not have snapped a cap at him."

The year's work on this field was a most fruitful one. The membership was doubled, and though the charge was not above the average in financial strength, he received the largest salary of any member of the conference.

Little attention was given, at this time, to the cause of missions. Money was not generally recognized as a vital factor in Christian service. Salaries were meager and often consisted in provisions rather than cash. In many places a strong sentiment prevailed against a paid ministry. Poverty and ignorance were considered necessary prerequisites to ministerial piety. The General Missionary Board was only about nine years old, and missionary sentiment had not taken deep root. But Newgent sowed missionary seed with a lavish hand, and had the pleasure of reaping at least part of the harvest. His ability to lead men to loosen their purse strings even then began to be asserted in a marked degree. More than half of the missionary contributions of the entire conference that year was reported from Brulitz Creek Circuit.

His report attracted attention and won him considerable distinction at the annual conference. According to custom each pastor reported in person in the open conference relative to the different interests of his charge. When asked about his missionary offering, Newgent replied, "Here it is," and taking a woolen bag, commonly called a sock, from his pocket he emptied its contents on the table. The contents consisted of coins of various denominations just as he had gathered them to the amount of $33.40, the small change giving it the appearance of a larger sum than he actually had.

However, this was considered remarkable. Most of the pastors reported nothing. Dr. D. K. Flickinger, the first missionary secretary of the Church, was occupying a seat on the platform near the Bishop, and joined heartily with him in applause at the splendid report and the unique manner of presenting it.

The year's work placed the "boy preacher" in a most favorable light, and led to his appointment to the Shawnee Prairie Circuit, the strongest charge in the Conference. The charge had had the pastoral service of Rev. Thomas H. Hamilton, a mighty man who stood high in the counsels of the denomination. It was characterized by more than the usual amount of wealth and culture, and withal an air of aristocracy that led to demands upon a pastor that were most exacting. Rev. Mr. Hamilton was a favorite on the circuit, and the people had no thought of losing him. His election to the office of presiding elder, however, necessitated the change, and when the awkward, and, as they thought, inexperienced lad came among them, they felt that their aristocratic tastes were outraged. It was a wet, chilly day in April when he arrived, and the crestfallen spirits of the people made it still more chilly for him. And when he learned that the matter of rejecting him was being seriously considered, the situation was anything but cheerful.

He told the people he would remain until the first quarterly meeting, when the presiding elder, Rev. Mr. Hamilton, would be present, and that he would willingly abide by their decision at that time. This was a judicious step, as it gave him an opportunity to prove himself. So he went to work with his usual zeal and by the time of the quarterly meeting he had sixty conversions with about an equal number of additions to the church. All thought of rejecting the pastor had completely vanished. In fact they would not have swapped him off for the "biggest gun they had ever heard fired." Such success as the charge had never known crowned the labors of that year—great revivals at all the appointments, the circuit more than doubled in strength, and enthusiasm at high tide. Thus their mourning was turned into laughing. A unanimous demand was made for his return for another year, but his restless spirit sought new worlds to conquer. His motto has always been that it is better to go to a needy field and build it up than to go where further advancement is impossible. On this ground he asked to be sent to a new field.

One experience on Shawnee Prairie Circuit is worthy of special mention. Contiguous to the circuit, near Attica in Fountain County, was a section of country known as Hell's Half Acre. Its leading spirit was an infidel doctor. His influence and teachings had so dominated the community that it was found impossible to maintain religious services there. Ministers were considered proud, indolent, and altogether an undesirable lot. Newgent determined to do some missionary work in that benighted place, though repeated efforts to that end had been made in vain.

In order to make a favorable impression and avoid the imprecation of being proud, he dressed in his everyday clothes and visited the district school, which was the geographical and social center, and the only place where meetings could be held. He announced that there would be services at the school house that evening, to be continued indefinitely, and urged the children to spread the news.

The announcement, however, did not produce satisfactory results. The attendance the first three or four evenings did not exceed a half-dozen. The atmosphere was rather chilly and the spiritual barometer did not indicate an early change. It soon became apparent that the old doctor was the key to the situation. If the people were to be reached, it must be done mainly through him. How to capture this Goliath was now the problem, and this problem Newgent set about to solve.

The Sunday services having been no better attended than the preceding ones, he decided upon a bold move. On Monday afternoon he called at the doctor's home. The doctor answered his knock at the door in person. The old fellow's rough demeanor and uncouth appearance, his ancient cob pipe that had long been entitled to a superannuated relation, the musty, dingy room which the half-open door disclosed—all seemed in striking harmony with his attitude toward religion. The preacher introduced himself and explained that he was holding a revival over at the school house. The grizzled old sinner looked him over from head to foot, but said nothing, though the expression on his sin-hardened face seemed to say more plainly than words, "Well, you little rascal, you had better be at home with your mother."

"I understand," persisted the preacher, ignoring the old gentleman's contemptuous frown, "that you are a good singer and a prominent citizen, and I would like to consult you about the work and get you to help me."

"Help in a revival? Why, don't you know that I don't believe in the Bible or churches, or religion of any sort?"

"Well, that needn't stand in the way. The evenings are long and the young people want somewhere to go. You can do the singing and I'll do the preaching."

The Boy Preacher Visiting the Infidel.

That put a different complexion on things. Here was a chance for some fun, and incidentally an outlet for his musical propensities, for he was well versed in music. The idea seemed to take hold. The grim features began to relax. The boys were called and told to "put up the preacher's horse," and the preacher was invited into the house. The invitation was heartily accepted. Newgent understood fishing; he had fished before. The hook was baited and he now perceived that he had got a nibble. The afternoon was spent to a good advantage. Conversation flowed in various channels, but fought shy of religion—no time for that yet. He waited for his fish to take the cork under before pulling in. The doctor had a large family of children, and their appearance bore testimony to the fact that they were strangers to church and Sunday school. The boys spread the startling news that "dad was goin' to help the boy preacher in the big meetin'." And such news traveled as it were with seven-leagued boots.

That was all the advertisement the meeting needed. The infidel accompanied the preacher to the meeting, taking his place up front, and led the singing after the droll manner then in vogue. An earthquake or a man from the dead would not have created more excitement or comment. From that time the little school house did not accommodate the crowds.

The sermon that evening was not calculated to create a very profound impression. It was more saturated with Irish humor than with real gospel truth. The time for seriousness had not yet arrived. But the axe was laid at the root of the tree, and the kingdom was nearer at hand than any of them supposed. As a fisher of men, the preacher was still baiting for the fish.

The next night he took for his theme the Judgment. This was the occasion for solemn and serious facts. He turned loose all the artillery at his command in storming the batteries of infidelity and sin, and felt the presence of the Spirit in directing the message. As he neared the close of his discourse, he turned to the doctor. The wind had been taken out of the old man's sails; his face was in his hands and he was weeping bitterly.

"What's the matter, doctor?" he shouted, in a strong, firm voice, striving to make his words as impressive as possible.

The doctor did not answer.

"Get down on your knees," he commanded as one who spoke with authority.

And the great exponent of infidelity went down, and his example was followed by a number of others. He wrestled in agony and prayer until near midnight, when the light broke in upon his long benighted soul—and the fish was caught. Such demonstrations had never been seen in Hell's Half Acre as took place in the rude school house that night. The tide had surely turned and the redemption was at hand.

As he dismissed the service, Newgent announced that he was ready to go home with the first man who invited him. A tall, threadbare, weather-beaten fellow accepted the challenge. But when the preacher started to go, he explained that he didn't mean it. "I can't take care of you; I haven't any room," he protested.

"Go ahead," said the preacher, "I can sleep on dry coon skins and eat roasted potatoes." And he went in spite of the protests of his host.

The man was surely honest in his protest. He dwelt in a hut built of round poles. In one corner was a badly cracked stove that had long done service for both cooking and heating purposes. Two large box-like arrangements partly filled with leaves gathered from the forest, together with some ragged covering, served as feeble apologies for beds, and between these beds was a barrel of whisky. Though it was past midnight, the wife was sitting up. She was scantily clad, yet her face, though careworn, revealed a high degree of intelligence, bearing evidence that she had seen better days. Two little girls whose appearance harmonized only too well with their wretched surroundings, completed the family circle. As Newgent entered this hovel his eyes rested upon such a picture of destitution as he had never seen. The whisky barrel, however, told the whole story.

Newgent soon had the entire family feeling perfectly at ease. He played with the children and proved himself a most congenial guest. But he was there for their spiritual good. That night the wretched home, for the first time, became a house of prayer. Before the light of a new day dawned the light from heaven broke in upon the sad heart of that wife and mother, and a new day dawned in her life. The next morning the husband likewise found the Savior, and the whisky barrel, the cause of so much misery and poverty, vacated its place in the home, for old things had passed away and all things had become new. Another stronghold was lost to the enemy. A glorious night's work it was, and a mighty step toward the final conquest of this spiritual Canaan.

The man asked Newgent to roll the barrel of whisky into the river. But he said, "No; let us sell it to the druggist. We can use the money to a good advantage." So he borrowed a team and wagon, and hauled the whisky to the nearest drug store, and received eighteen dollars for it. With the money he bought some much needed clothing for the wife and children. It was his first and only experience in the whisky business.

The entire community was swept by the revival. Multitudes were converted, a church was organized, and a church-house built. The whisky man and the ex-infidel became pillars in the church, one serving as class leader and the other as steward. Never was a work of grace more complete, or the power of God more wonderfully or graciously displayed in the transformation of a community than in the case of Hell's Half Acre.

CHAPTER FIVE.

Six Months at Rainsville—A Hotbed of Southern Sympathizers—A Mix-up with Saloon Men—A Sermon on Slavery—Fire and Brimstone—An Antagonist Outwitted—A Sermon from the Book of Newgent—Can Any Good Thing Come Out of Rainsville?

In 1861, the time of holding the Upper Wabash Conference was changed from spring to fall. Hence, two sessions were held that year with an interim of but six months between them. This period was spent by Rev. Mr. Newgent on the Williamsport Circuit in Warren County, Indiana. He moved with his family to Rainsville, a village of about one hundred and fifty inhabitants, located on Vermilion River. The town was still in the rough, its chief activities centering about two rival saloons. As it had no church and not a single inhabitant who professed religion, the saloons had things pretty much their own way. The Newgents occupied part of a building that formerly did service as the village inn; the rest of it was occupied by one of the saloon keepers. The two families, however, did not have undisputed possession of the place, as it seemed to have been preempted by bed bugs and fleas, which were no inconspicuous feature of life in Rainsville. While the saloon keeper and the preacher maintained peaceable relations with each other, these aboriginal neighbors maintained an attitude of hostility with a persistence that was worthy of a better cause than they represented.

Another thing that made life in Rainsville interesting during this period was the war which was then in its first year of progress. The sympathies of the inhabitants were decidedly with the South. But one man could be found who claimed to be loyal to the Union, and as might be expected under such circumstances, he was not very enthusiastic about it. They could safely be counted on the off side of any question or movement that involved a moral element. With the war agitation to stir their blood, the well patronized saloons doing business seven days and nights in the week, and the absence of any religious institution or influence, Rainsville might well have served as a basis for the doctrine of total depravity.

The Williamsport Circuit, like most of the country parishes of its day, afforded a man plenty of room to grow in. If a pastor rusted out it was his own fault. But Newgent, with his active temperament and fondness for adventure, was not the man to rust out. Not only the Sabbath, but most of the evenings between Sabbaths were taken up with preaching services. Each alternate Sabbath during the Williamsport pastorate he preached four times, which entailed forty-two miles of travel by horseback. The day's program was as follows: Leaving home at daybreak, he rode twenty miles to a ten o'clock appointment. After the service he would get a "hand out" for dinner and reach the next appointment at two o'clock, then to a 4:30 service, and on home for meeting at night. Life was both simple and strenuous in the extreme.

The first Sunday in this village was a memorable one. Leaving his plucky young wife to hold the fort, the new pastor made his forty-two-mile round, reaching home about sundown. No provision had been made for preaching in town, but Newgent resolved to give the inhabitants of this inferno a chance to hear the gospel. A rowdy mob was collected about each saloon. An air of general lawlessness, recklessness, and cussedness prevailed. Games and sports of various sorts were maintained on the streets. Horseback riders were galloping here and there, firing pistols and performing various stunts in imitation of life among the untamed cowboys and Indians. Their boisterous talking and hollowing, with here and there a man staggering under his load of Rainsville's chief product, all combined, might well have led to the conclusion that the demons of the lower regions had been liberated and were holding high carnival in celebration of the event.

When Newgent told his wife that he had decided to preach at the school house that night, she tried to dissuade him, fearing for his safety. And well she might after what she had seen of life in Rainsville that day. But he gloried in heroic tasks and heeded not her wise counsel. He at once set about to publish the appointment. In order to find the people he went to one of the saloons. The saloon was full of men, and the men were full of the saloon. Stepping up to the bar-tender he told him that he was going to hold a religious service at the school house at 7:30. "As there are no church services in town," he said, "I am sure you will be willing to encourage such a movement by closing your place of business and attending."

"You can preach all you d—— please; I haven't been to church for twenty years," answered the booze dispenser with a look that seemed to add, "and I don't propose to commence now."

"But I am a stranger here, and you don't know but I am the smartest man in the country, or may be the biggest fool. You had better come and find out for yourself."

The idea of a church service struck the saloon patrons as a desirable innovation, and as they were in favor of anything that promised a diversion, they began to take sides with the preacher. Their enthusiasm waxed intense, due mainly to the reflex influence of tarrying long at the grog shop. They were unanimous and emphatic in demanding that the saloon be closed and that all go to church.

The proprietor finally said that he would consent on condition that his competitor would do likewise.

"All right, I'll see him," and Newgent broke for the other saloon where a similar situation prevailed. Several of the men volunteered to accompany him and assist in enforcing the demand, so that an ambassage that carried with it no small authority presented itself before the high priest of Gambrinus of the rival saloon. A delegation from one saloon to another, headed by a preacher, was an uncommon sight, especially in Rainsville, but it had the desired effect. For once the saloons were closed and the center of interest transferred to the school house. News of the meeting spread in short order. The new preacher made himself an object of curiosity and comment by his establishing diplomatic relations with the governing bodies of the village, and everybody was anxious to see more of him. So all Rainsville turned out to church—men, women, boys, girls, and dogs—all entering heartily into the novelty of a religious service with a real, "sure enough" preacher at the head of it.

Newgent prudently made the service brief. The sermon was not as spiritual as it might have been under different conditions, as the congregation was quite sympathetic and responsive, and he considered it injudicious to encourage their emotions at that time. He was more especially concerned about laying plans for the future. How to get them back was the question, which he sought to solve by a bit of strategy. So, in addition to giving them a few morsels of wholesome advice, well sugarcoated with his native good humor, he made the startling announcement that at the next meeting he would preach on the subject of slavery. If anything were calculated to bring them back, surely that was.

It was taken for granted, of course, that he was an Abolitionist and would denounce the South. The blood of those southern sympathizers at once began to boil. Everybody anticipated a lively time, and interest became intense. All felt that the foolhardy young fellow did not realize the danger to which he was exposing himself. An old gentleman, the village blacksmith, whose father had been a United Brethren preacher, felt it his duty to warn the reverend gentleman and have him to call off the entire proceedings. As usual, Newgent was firm. He told the gentleman, however, that he wanted to be fair to both sides, so if those who disagreed with him desired, they might get a man to follow him and present the other side of the question.

This they were only too anxious to do. When the time came, they had their man. By the time Newgent and his wife arrived at the little school house that evening it was completely packed and an immense crowd was gathered on the outside. It was with the greatest difficulty that they forced themselves through the anxious throng and made their way to the front of the building. The opponent was on hand, ready to take his measure and smash all of his arguments. As might be surmised, sympathy was plainly and emphatically with the southern advocate. If he could not demolish the frail Abolitionist, there were enough present who were ready to lend all the assistance he needed. The smell of brimstone was in the air, indicating the presence of that commodity in unlimited quantities. All that was lacking for a real conflagration was something to touch it off. And that something was momentarily expected.

After a brief preliminary exercise, the preacher opened the discussion. Like the great apostle on Mars Hill, he complimented his hearers on their seeming interest in the subject at hand. "As the subject of slavery," he said, "is stirring our country from one end to the other, and as it is a subject of such vital importance, I take pleasure at this time in presenting one phase of it.

"I wish to observe in my remarks, First, the slave; Second, his master; Third, the law by which he is held in bondage; Fourth, how he is to be liberated; Fifth, where he is to be colonized." Thus far, well and good. These were familiar topics, and had been discussed pro and con even by the school children. Hence, his opening remarks were according to expectations, and breathlessly they awaited what was to follow.

Their consternation and chagrin can only be imagined when he proceeded to state that the slave is the sinner; his master is the devil; the law by which he is held in bondage is sinful lusts and habits; he is to be liberated through the blood of Christ; and heaven is the place of his colonization. Around these propositions he built his discourse without any reference to slavery as a civil institution. It was strictly a gospel sermon, and his antagonist had no disposition to reply.

"Well, we are beat," said the old blacksmith after the service was dismissed, "but the boy is the sharpest fellow that ever struck this town." And he was not alone in his conclusion.

With a view to holding the audience for the next appointment, he announced that he would preach at that time from the Book of Newgent, the twenty-eighth chapter and thirty-third verse, "Can any good thing come out of Rainsville?"

A few days after this announcement, he received a call from an old gentleman. The unsuspecting brother had been having trouble over the Book of Newgent. He stated that he and the old woman had been searching the Bible all week and were unable to find it. He was kindly urged to be present at the preaching service and assured that his troubles would all be cleared up. Presumably the matter was explained to his satisfaction, as he was not heard from again.

The Rainsville pastorate, though brief, was full of thrilling interest, and was not without substantial results for good. He won the respect and confidence of this uncouth people, and had the satisfaction of seeing many of the grosser evils disappear under his ministry. Before he left, the signs of a brighter day were plainly discernible. His influence with them was turned to good account, as will be seen in the next chapter.

CHAPTER SIX.

The War Spirit in Indiana—Breaking up a Traitorous Plot—Narrow Escape from Enemies—Assists in Securing Recruits—Becomes Chaplain of his Regiment—Exchange of Courtesies with a Presbyterian Minister—An Embarrassing Predicament—Saves Regiment from Capture—Organizes a Military Church—Chased by Johnnies—An Exciting Homeward Journey.

Indiana was a storm center during the Civil War. Her position was a strategic one. She was regarded as the keystone of the North. With Oliver P. Morton, "Indiana's great War Governor," at the head of affairs, she was held firmly to her moorings, and furnished a larger number of soldiers for the Union Army in proportion to population than any other State. Yet the State was constantly harassed by citizens who were unfriendly to the Union cause, and who secretly or openly sympathized with the South. Secret organizations for the purpose of aiding the Confederacy were common. Conspicuous among these was the Knights of the Golden Circle. Yet many not identified with these traitorous organizations were utterly disloyal. Hence, much bitterness and not infrequently bloodshed prevailed. It was not unusual for men in official position to use their influence against the Government, or even to join the army with traitorous intent.

Rev. Mr. Newgent was serving as pastor for the second year on the Clark's Hill charge, when in the fall of 1863, he was "persuaded," as he said, "to go into the army for safety." With his wife he was paying a visit to his father-in-law in Parke County. In the neighborhood lived a man who was captain of Home Guards, but whose loyalty was strongly suspected. A small brother of Mrs. Newgent sometimes visited with his children, and on returning from one such visit, incidentally mentioned having seen some pretty guns in the barn where they had been playing. Newgent understood the meaning of these guns secreted on the premises of this traitorous man, and telegraphed the news to Governor Morton. A squad of soldiers was dispatched to the place and some three hundred guns were found. They were confiscated and a traitorous scheme was thus frustrated.

Newgent at once became the object of a great deal of attention. That he was responsible for the exposure, was generally surmised. A plan was formed to do away with him. On Sunday evening following the episode he was to preach at the Oak Ridge United Brethren Church in the community. In the midst of the service, by a preconcerted plan, the lights were suddenly extinguished, and his adversaries were about to execute their design. He succeeded in making his escape in the darkness by the assistance of an uncle. The outlook seemed rather stormy, and he was convinced that it was safer in the army than out of it. Leaving his wife in the care of her father, he hastened to Lafayette where a regiment, the 116th Indiana Infantry, was being formed by Colonel William C. Kise.

At that period recruits were hard to get and the work proceeded slowly. Newgent asked the colonel what the chance would be for him to get the appointment of chaplain.

"What church do you belong to?" the colonel asked.

"I am a United Brethren," was the answer.

"I am sorry," said the colonel, "I like the United Brethren Church and would like to give you the appointment; but this is to be a Methodist regiment; all the officers are to be Methodists, and it is understood that the chaplainship is to be given to a Methodist preacher up in the city."

"Will you take me, then, as a private?" he asked.

"Certainly," was the eager reply, "we shall be glad to take you, for recruits are coming in awfully slowly." There were then only seven companies started. None of them were complete. Newgent offered to assist in raising recruits.

"If you will give me transportation papers," he said, "I think I can get some men over in Warren County."

"Warren County!" exclaimed the colonel in disgust. "It's of no use to go there for recruits. I have had a couple of good men over there for three weeks and they have got only four men." But Newgent insisted that he be allowed to try. He understood those people and felt that he knew how to approach them. The papers were finally given him, and he set out for Rainsville in this doubtful territory.

Rainsville, it will be remembered, was a headquarters for southern sympathizers, where little more than a year before but one Union man could be found. The task was a challenge to Newgent, the kind of a task he delighted in. Taking a boy with a drum and flag, he went to the village and nearby points, and soon had the inhabitants inoculated with the war microbe. The prospects of a draft about this time proved an effective argument in favor of enlistment, which was used for all it was worth. After an absence of six days he returned to camp with 104 men, which was the first full company in the regiment, this, too, from territory that was as completely southern in sentiment as though it had been in the very heart of the Confederacy.

The march to camp was a triumphal procession. The company of volunteers was accompanied by several hundred men and boys who fell in on the way. As they came into camp about twelve o'clock on Saturday night with colors flying and giving vent to their enthusiasm by singing and hollowing, it had the effect of a small army, not unlike that of Gideon's band, when they multiplied the effect of numbers by noise and enthusiasm and scared the Midianites out of their wits. The colonel met them with a drum corps and the company was welcomed amid the most extravagant expressions of delight. The fact that recruits were coming in so slowly gave increased cause for demonstration. When the general hubbub had somewhat abated, the crowd demanded a speech from Newgent, and the demand was imperative. Though worn by physical exertion and hoarse from much haranguing, he gave a brief talk, at the close of which, amid great applause, some one moved that "Rev. Mr. Newgent be made chaplain of the regiment." It was heartily seconded, and shouts of approval burst from every section of the camp. So, by general consent the rule to make it a Methodist regiment was waived, insofar as it related to the chaplainship, much to the satisfaction of Colonel Kise, and Newgent became their spiritual adviser.

The Methodist brother, who, it was understood, was to receive the appointment, came out the next afternoon (Sunday) to preach to the boys and get acquainted; but on being apprised of what had taken place the night before, he quietly withdrew, leaving Newgent in undisputed possession of the honors which his tact and energy had won.

The regiment was finally completed and mustered in for a term of six months, though it served considerably over time. Its first service was rendered in guarding the U. S. Armory at Detroit, Michigan. The armory was threatened by General Vallandigham, who had been banished from the United States because of treasonable expressions, and had placed himself at the head of a force in Canada with the purpose of threatening the Union from the north. The regiment was later sent to reënforce General Burnsides in east Tennessee.

This was during the terrible winter of '63 and '64, when Burnsides was besieged by Confederate General Longstreet and was shut up in Knoxville. The hardships suffered by the Union soldiers during that memorable siege are matters of history and need not be recounted in detail here. Among the foremost of the sufferers was Newgent's regiment, the 116th Indiana. All supplies having been cut off, the boys for many weeks had a hard struggle to keep from succumbing to hunger and cold. For a time they each had but one ear of corn a day; no tents, and not sufficient clothing for protection even under favorable circumstances. In the midst of the severest winter weather, over three hundred of the men were barefooted. Newgent was the best dressed man in his regiment, and it was with difficulty that he got his dress coat to hang together at the collar; and he suffered no little uneasiness lest his trousers would dissolve partnership with him.

A few characteristic army experiences will suffice in this connection and occupy the remainder of this chapter.

On reaching Tennessee, the regiment was stationed temporarily at Greenville. The care-free boys attended services the first Sunday morning at the Presbyterian church in the city. The pastor, Rev. Samuel McCorkle, treated them kindly. They were delighted with the reception accorded them, and on the following Sabbath a large part of the regiment, including the chaplain, turned out to worship at Rev. Mr. McCorkle's church. When Newgent appeared in his chaplain's uniform, McCorkle at once led him up to the pulpit and insisted that he preach. The chaplain was never averse to preaching whenever there was occasion for it, and so consented, under slight pressure. He observed the pastor's manuscript neatly tied up with red ribbon, which told him he had barely escaped listening to a manuscript sermon. Newgent had little sympathy for a written discourse and took advantage of the situation to indulge in some pleasantries at the learned parson's expense. He told the congregation, the greater part of whom were soldiers, that he had no set discourse, and that he never tried to palm off a written sermon upon a helpless congregation, as such a procedure was "like a doctor writing a prescription before examining the patient." Rev. Mr. McCorkle accepted the criticism good-naturedly and invited Newgent to take dinner with him after the service. After several weeks of army rations, the dinner at Rev. Mr. McCorkle's home was a most delightful change.

He returned the courtesy that had been accorded him by inviting his host to preach to his "boys" in the afternoon. The invitation was accepted. McCorkle did not deem it judicious to use his manuscript after the episode of the forenoon, and was visibly handicapped and embarrassed in his attempt at extemporaneous delivery. He talked but a few minutes and turned the service over to the chaplain.

After the service the two men had a heart-to-heart talk. McCorkle confessed his chagrin at not being able to preach without his manuscript, and expressed a determination to cultivate the habit of extemporaneous delivery. That the determination was carried out was seen in the fact that he became a leader in this method of preaching. And the two preachers continued fast friends.

An incident more pleasing to relate than to undergo occurred at Tazewell, Tennessee, where Newgent's regiment had been dispatched with twenty-four others to check a Confederate force that was approaching from that quarter. They went into camp, building temporary fortifications with the grave stones of a nearby cemetery. About midnight the army was surprised by the sudden arrival of a force of Confederate cavalry that captured some of the outposts. Newgent, with some of his regiment, was garrisoned in an old building that had been used for a granary. As the fire was opened he caught up his clothes in his arms, and, mounting his horse, started down the hill for a more healthful location. The horse stumbled over some rocks, throwing the rider to the ground and scattering his precious wearing apparel to the four winds. There was no time for trifles, and the clothes were abandoned for the time. They were recovered about nine o'clock the next morning, much to the relief of the reverend, whose situation in the meantime was as embarrassing as it was uncomfortable.

On one occasion his coolness and ingenuity were the means of saving his entire regiment from capture. The regiment had been ordered across the Clinch River in east Tennessee to guard a narrow passage in the mountains at what was called Bean's Station. They had gotten across and were camping in a bend of the river when news came that the rebels had superseded them, and three brigades were between them and the gap. They might easily have retreated, but the river became swollen from heavy rains, and to cross a swift, mountain stream under such circumstances was practically out of the question.

Newgent was sick at the time, being cared for at the colonel's headquarters. During the early part of the night the colonel came to him, trembling with fear, and said, "Chaplain, what on earth is to be done? There is a strong rebel force on one side of us, and an unfordable stream on the other. If we are not out of here by morning every one of us will be captured."

The rebels were confident that they could not get away and so waited until morning to bag their game.

"Bring six or seven of the boys here," said Newgent. The boys were brought. He told them to go down to the river where they would find an old canoe partly filled with water. "Build a fire on the bank so that its light will shine across the stream, bail the water out of the canoe, put it in as good shape as possible, and then report."

They followed his instructions, after which they came back to headquarters, and the sick chaplain got out of his bed and went back with them to the river. Though it was a perilous undertaking, the men got in the water-soaked canoe, and by the uncertain light of the fire, made their way to the other side of the angry stream. They went to General Curtain's headquarters, related the situation, and procured a supply of cannon rope. With the rope they made a cable across the river. They thus devised a rude ferry by means of an abandoned and partly submerged barge which they raised and repaired for the purpose. The barge would carry about twelve men or one horse at a trip. It was propelled by the men holding to the cable and thus laboriously working their way from one side of the stream to the other. Through the dark, stormy night they toiled, and before daybreak the entire regiment with all appurtenances was out of reach of the enemy. When the rebels reached forth their hand next morning to bag their game, lo! it wasn't there!

It was a terrible night's work, however. The sick chaplain stayed with the barge until the last man was saved. He was twice thrown into the water, and ran a fearful risk in thus exposing himself at so critical a time. After the excitement of the night, by which alone his physical strength was sustained, he suffered a serious relapse. He was confined to his bed at General Curtain's headquarters for about two weeks, when he again reported for duty. The men regarded him as their deliverer, and the satisfaction of having saved his comrades from the horrors of a southern prison compensated for all he suffered. For this heroic deed he was complimented on dress parade by a special order from the general.

The following reference to this incident is found in the "Official Records of the Army," Series I., Vol. XXXI.:

Tazewell, Tenn., December 14, 1863.

Major-General Foster, Knoxville:

General: I have the honor of reporting that I arrived here this evening at about dark, having left Rutledge at 9:00 a. m., and Bean's Station at 1:30 p. m.... At the crossing of the Clinch River (Evan's Ford) I found a sufficient guard, under the command of Colonel Kise. The river was rising quite rapidly, but the guard had raised and repaired the ferry-boat, which was crossing successfully, being pulled back and forth by hand upon a cable stretched from one shore to another. I think that it would be well, as a matter of security, to have another boat built there, and will so notify Colonel Babcock....

I am, general, very respectfully, your obedient servant,

O. M. POE,
Captain and Chief Engineer, Army of the Ohio.

As a means for the spiritual welfare of the "boys," he conceived and carried out the idea of organizing a military church. Though there were various religious organizations among the soldiers, and some doubtless on similar lines, yet this was an entirely original conception with him. His church took no denominational name, but was made up of all who were willing to become members. It was completely officered, and maintained prayer meetings and church services at stated intervals. Two special revival meetings were held in which about 250 of the "boys" were converted.

His spiritual ministrations were not limited to the soldiers. Whenever an opportunity presented itself he would hold services at nearby churches and school houses. On one such occasion he incidentally, to use his own expression, "chased seven Johnnies for three and a half miles." It was a merry race; like Jehu the entire party rode furiously. But as the chaplain had more at stake than his companions in the chase, he managed to maintain his position well in advance of the seven, and was quite willing to abandon the chase by the time he reached camp.

Not least among the interesting army "experiences" was the homeward journey. As previously stated, the regiment served over the time for which they enlisted. The men were impatient and homesick. Their destitute condition rendered many of them almost desperate. Almost half of them were barefooted and all were weakened by hunger and exposure. The morning on which they were to start home the colonel announced that they would proceed to Barbersville, Kentucky, and that there they would find a supply of much-needed clothing and provisions. This was a two-days' march, which, in itself, was no pleasing prospect under the circumstances. The promise of food and clothing, however, nerved them for the ordeal. It was midnight when Barbersville was reached, and to their utter consternation the promised supplies were not there.

Things were looking blue. The colonel said to Newgent, "You have the best horse in the regiment. Take a couple of the boys and get out and find something to feed these men before morning." He started, not to forage, but to beg. At the first house he came to be was met by a woman to whom he stated his mission. She showed him a blood spot on the floor where her husband had been killed by the rebels, and said that all she had was a half-bushel of meal, but she was willing to divide. It was all he secured, though he continued the search until daylight. Returning to camp, he threw the bit of meal at the colonel's feet, and fell down exhausted, dropping at once into a deep sleep.

What happened during the time he slept, when the real situation dawned upon the men, he could only surmise. The next he knew, the colonel had him aroused and was ordering him to ride ahead of the regiment to a little water-mill about twelve miles distant to see what could be found there, and to arrange if possible to feed the men when they arrived. He found a few bushels of grain, most of it in a bad condition. When ground into meal it made just one pint each for the men. After they had eaten their morsel, the colonel made them a little speech in which he told them that the next objective point would be Camp Dick Robinson, and for every man to look out for himself until they reached the camp. This they were quite glad to do. And when in a few days they met at the camp, they were in better spirits, and were pretty well supplied for the rest of the journey.

The next way station was Camp Nelson. Here they were met by the Provost Marshal who declared the regiment under arrest for pillaging, and ordered them to stack arms. While the authorities were arranging the details for taking care of them, the colonel took advantage of the delay. "Attention, Battalions," he shouted, "Shoulder arms—forward march—double quick!" The order was eagerly obeyed. A "double-quick" march was made to Nicholasville. This was a railroad town. Here they ordered a train for Cincinnati. The train steamed out of the station with its load of animated freight just as the Marshal with his guard galloped in sight.

The authorities at Cincinnati were notified by wire to arrest the regiment on its arrival there, but this was anticipated. So they got off the train at Covington, crossing the Ohio River by ferry to Cincinnati. There they got a train for Indianapolis without being detected. The train was pressed into service to convey them on to Lafayette, the home of the regiment. They reached the city on Sunday evening, as the church bells were ringing for the evening services. Newgent, as his custom was, went to church. Possibly he felt the need of it after what he had gone through. He went to the First Methodist Episcopal Church, and at the urgent request of the pastor, delivered the evening discourse to the delight of the splendid audience.

It should be said in justice to Rev. Mr. Newgent that he was not a party to any of the irregularities that almost brought his regiment into disrepute after it had acquitted itself so well on the field. He remonstrated with the men and exhorted them to better conduct, but when the pressure of army discipline was removed, the pent-up energies of these raw backwoodsmen were turned loose along various channels and could neither be suppressed nor regulated. The officers of the regiment, with the exception of Newgent, were summoned before the proper military tribunal at Indianapolis, to answer for their depredations. They were acquitted, however, being ably defended by Lieutenant-Colonel G. O. Beam. Whether or not the verdict was a just one, is of no special concern to us here. Suffice it to say that our subject, though a young man, so ordered his life as not only to keep himself unspotted from the world, but at the same time to win for himself the confidence of even the most hardened sinners. He was exonerated from all blame in advance, and his name was not brought before the court.

CHAPTER SEVEN.

Plants the United Brethren Banner in Terre Haute—Prairieton Pastorate—Difficulty with the Sons of Anak—A Prayer Without an "Amen"—Another Community Redeemed—Going to the Wrong Doctor—A Perverse Colt—An Unintentional Immersion—One Sermon That was not Dry.

It was in April, 1864, when Rev. Mr. Newgent returned from the war. His own conference did not meet until fall, but the Lower Wabash Conference met in its annual session in Vermilion, Illinois, about the time of his return. With the view to getting back on the firing line at once, he attended the latter conference, and was appointed to Terre Haute (Indiana) Mission. This was strictly prospective work, as the mission was projected at this session. The conference at the same session, following the example of the Upper Wabash Conference, decided to change the time of its annual meetings from spring to fall, hence the appointment was made for a period of only six months. During this time Rev. Mr. Newgent devoted himself with characteristic zeal to laying broad and deep the foundations of his church in this new Macedonia. That his labors were fruitful is seen in the fact that he reported to the fall conference an organized church on Second Street, with splendid prospects of a prosperous future—prospects which subsequent history has abundantly fulfilled. To him belongs the credit of first planting the United Brethren banner in this thriving city, where the Church has since steadily grown to a place of prestige and influence.

The Terre Haute pastorate was followed by a year at Prairieton, in Vigo County, Indiana. Some experiences on this field are worthy of note. A revival meeting was held in an unevangelized community at what was known as the Battle Row School House, near the Wabash River. The school house was a primitive log building with plenty of ventilation. The wide cracks between the logs in the walls not only admitted a sufficiency of fresh air, but were a source of temptation to the untamed sons of the natives who were wont at critical times to inject missiles of various sorts through them into the midst of the congregation, causing more or less uneasiness and often confusion to the worshipers. It was not a place where one could worship under his own vine and fig tree with no one to molest or make afraid. During the early stage of the meeting reapers were scarce, and to all appearances, were wholly inadequate to the demands of the great, over-ripe harvest. The sons of Anak seemed to have a perpetual title to the place, and showed no intention of evacuating it. At one time, as Newgent was making an earnest plea for penitents to come to the altar, he observed a company of ruffians in the rear of the room in a rather impenitent condition, bantering one another to go forward to the mourner's bench. The quick wit of the preacher frustrated their evil designs. Constant vigilance had to be exercised to prevent outbreaks and demonstrations of a similar character. As the meeting proceeded converts multiplied and the odds became more and more to the advantage of the faithful.

There was one wheel-horse who was the pastor's right hand man in the great conflict with primitive elements. A splendid man he was, though his droll manner was a subject of sport for the lewd fellows of the baser propensities. A characteristic attitude when he offered public prayer was to kneel facing the wall, with his back toward the congregation. Then with his eyes closed and oblivious to all his surroundings, he would soar to a high altitude in his eloquence and fervency of spirit. In such surroundings, however, it would have been better had Father Scott, as he was affectionately called, not forgotten his relation to this mundane sphere, for the situation surely demanded watching as well as praying. Especially would it have prevented an awkward hitch in the services one evening when the interest and enthusiasm were at their greatest height. Intense conviction was capturing and humbling proud and defiant hearts, and victory was perching upon the banners of the loyal band.

But, as in the days of Job, when the sons of God went to worship, Satan went also. Battle Row School House furnished a good demonstration of the fact that,

"Wherever God erects a house of prayer,

The devil's sure to build a chapel there;

And 'twill be found upon investigation,

The latter has by far the larger congregation."

While the worshipers were in the midst of great rejoicing, Satan's hosts were holding high carnival on the outside. Father Scott was called upon, as he frequently was, at the most critical stage in the meeting, to lead in prayer. As his custom was, he knelt with his face to the wall, and by chance his mouth was dangerously near a huge crack. While sailing away in the ether world, and the people were hanging breathlessly upon his earnest and eloquent words, all unexpectedly, for some strange reason, the machinery stopped. It was unusual for a prayer to be terminated so abruptly without the conventional "amen." All eyes were fixed upon Father Scott. What could have happened? It was painfully apparent that he was in distress. He was making a desperate effort to clear some obstruction from his throat, get his breath, and regain his equilibrium.

The proximity of Father Scott's mouth to the opening in the wall was too great a provocation for the unregenerates on the outside of the house to forego. One of them had prepared a ball of mud, and with accurate aim, threw it through the crack into the brother's mouth, putting him temporarily out of commission. There was, of course, confusion in the midst of Zion, but Father Scott, whose battery had been silenced by this unexpected maneuver, was soon able to resume operations, and the battle was pressed with increased vigor.

A Prayer Without An Amen.

There was another neglected community adjacent to this charge. It was entirely without church services or religious influences of any kind. In the community lived a well-to-do gentleman of the name of Owen, whose wife was an invalid. Being of a religious turn of mind, and deprived of church privileges, she desired to have a meeting held at her home mainly for her benefit. Rev. Mr. Newgent was invited to conduct the service. His Sundays being taken up by his regular work, the meeting was held in a forenoon during the week. A goodly company of neighbors gathered out of respect to the dear sister, and she enjoyed the occasion so much that she invited them all back for a service in the evening. The evening meeting proved still more interesting, and it was decided to continue the services indefinitely. It developed into a grand revival which resulted in many conversions, the organization of a church, and the building of a church-house. Among the first to come to the mourner's bench was Mr. Owen, the generous host. He "came through" shouting and became a strong, staunch, and stormy defender of the faith.

Among attendants at the revival were two brothers, "Dave" and "Joe" Walker, notable characters in a local way. Both were proficient in the use of the violin, or, in the vernacular of the day, they were great fiddlers. Even if there was nothing else to place them under the ban of pious sentiment, this in itself would have been sufficient, for the fiddle had been so exclusively associated with bad company that it was supposed to have absorbed something of the evil spirits of its companions, and in the superstitious imaginations of many it possessed invisible hoofs and horns, and a strange, infernal power that was to be zealously avoided. Hence, Dave and Joe were regarded as typical "hard nuts," and it cannot be denied that they made an honest effort to live up to their reputations. They were more familiar with the conventionalities of the country "hoe-down" than with the atmosphere of a "big meetin'." Until the revival at the Owen home attracted their attention, they had not been present at a church service since they were boys. They became fairly regular attendants at the meeting, and in consequence, both got sick. Their illness seemed to be of a peculiar character, as neither of them could explain his symptoms or give any clue as to the seat of the trouble.

Joe became much worse one evening and by midnight he began to think he was being beckoned across the border. Dave, whose condition was not so critical, was dispatched to Prairieton for medical aid. While he was gone, Joe got religion. This proved to be all the treatment he needed. All unfavorable symptoms disappeared, and he set out post haste to meet his brother. Just before he reached the village, he met Dave on his way home, when the following colloquy took place:

"Oh, Dave, I've got all the medicine I need. It ain't pills we need, but religion."

"Bless the Lord, I've took the medicine, too," said Dave. He had also been converted on his return from the doctor's office. It thus became apparent that their malady was spiritual rather than physical, but being unfamiliar with symptoms of that character, they were unable to diagnose the case until the remedy had been applied. The two brothers were made every whit whole, soul and body. They hung up "the fiddle and the bow," and their talents and energies were turned loose along more legitimate channels.

Vermilion Circuit, in Illinois, was the scene of the next pastorate. Here a memorable experience took place as he was making his second "round" on the charge. Newgent, like other strong men, has always had some hobbies, legitimate hobbies in his case, however, that were elements of strength in his ministry. One of these is punctuality. He has always been scrupulously punctual in meeting his engagements. He never misses a train from the fact that he is far more likely to be at the station three-quarters of an hour ahead of time than three-quarters of a minute late. He is a strict believer in the maxim of the muse,

"Better be an hour early and stand and wait,

Than to be a moment behind the time."

In filling appointments he observes the same rule. He finds it helpful to be on hand sufficiently early to meet and shake hands with the advance guards of the congregation. It affords a tonic for his wits and puts him in a mood to be at his best.

On his new charge was a church known as Prairie Chapel. As usual, in his introductory services he exhorted his people to be punctual in their attendance, stating that he made it a point to be on time, and that if he at any time was not strictly "on the dot," they might know that something was wrong. It so happened that at the very next service the scrupulously punctual preacher was behind time, and it also happened that something was desperately wrong.

As a sort of background to the scene to be here presented, it would be well to state that he was clad in a new suit, as preachers usually were at the beginning of the year. The new suit consisted of a complete outfit from boots to hat and gloves, including also that luxury which not every circuit rider could afford, a fine shawl. It should further be explained that he was riding a colt, not the nineteen-year-old variety with which he traveled his first circuit, but a genuine three-year-old, with all the fire and perverseness of its kind. It might also be in order to add, by way of parenthesis, that the Illinois roads after the rains and frosts of September began their maneuvers, were no respecters of new clothes.

Just before reaching Prairie Chapel, the road crossed a slough some three hundred feet wide. At this point the road was covered by about three feet of water, or perhaps, as it was difficult to tell just where the water left off and the mud began, it would be more exact to say that it was three feet from the top of the water to the bottom of the mud. It was covered with a thin coating of ice. Newgent, being the first to pass that way on that Sunday morning, had to break the ice as he went. The colt did not like the task to begin with, but as this was the only road to the church and was fenced on either side with a picket fence, a straightforward course was the only alternative.

The colt proceeded reluctantly until it reached the middle of the slough. There it became possessed with the spirit of Balam's beast and refused to go farther. Its purpose seemed to be fixed as all the entreaties of the rider were unavailing. The church was in plain view, and, like the wedding guest of Coleridge's immortal "Rime," the preacher could see and hear the people as they were assembling, while he was transfixed to the spot. Finally giving up hope of going forward, he tried to turn the colt's head in the opposite direction, when, lo, he found that it was as averse to turning back as it was to going forward. Just what the beast's plan for the future was, could not well be divined, for, to be in the middle of a lake with no purpose of going either forward or backward was, to say the least, a position difficult to explain or defend. The final bell rang for the morning service, and the preacher began to realize that his reputation for punctuality was in danger of being water-soaked. A final desperate effort was made to induce locomotion, but to no avail.

It was a real Slough of Despond. The reverend's heart sank to the bottom of his new boots when he found that his only chance was to dismount. This he proceeded to do, supposing that he could at least lead the beast out of the water. The water was by no means comfortable, the mud filled his boots, and apprehensive thoughts concerning the unpresentable appearance he would make at church, and the damage being done to his new suit, and at the same time the humiliation of being beaten out by a perverse colt, all together did not tend to a devotional frame of mind.

An Unintentional Immersion.

Taking the rein, he waded forward, expecting the colt to follow, but it had no disposition to be led; he gave the rein a sharp pull, but the animal also had scruples against being pulled. He then gave the rein a jerk, putting all of his physical strength, and possibly a bit of his temper into the jerk, when, lo! the rein broke, and the preacher, not thinking of such a contingency, went splash into the water, being completely submerged. Things were rapidly going from bad to worse. It was of no use under the circumstances, to try to maintain ministerial dignity. Gathering himself together, he made his way to the fence, and, loosing a picket, he got behind the animal, and with a few strokes where they would do the most good, and unministerial maneuvers, he got it started, and by an aggressive follow-up campaign, they reached the shore without further ceremony or delay.

He hastened on to the church. The people were waiting for the belated pastor, and when he arrived, they saw at once there had been a valid excuse for his tardiness. There were four other ministers present, and Newgent tried to get one of them to preach in his stead, but all declined. So he went on with the regular program, and preached with his usual zeal while the water was still dripping from his new suit. It was one time at least when the congregation was not bored with a dry preacher.

After service he went home with one of his members, borrowed some dry clothes, and proceeded to fill his other appointments for the day.

CHAPTER EIGHT.

The New Goshen Pastorate—An Old Grudge Healed—Dry Bones Revived—Memorable Year at "Dogtown"—"Death in the Pot"—The Hittites Captured—The "Jerks"—Other Remarkable Demonstrations—A Rooster in the Missionary Collection—First Debate—Unpleasant Sequel to a Horse Trade.

Following the Vermilion pastorate, two years were spent on the New Goshen Circuit in Vigo County, Indiana. This circuit had ranked among the best in the conference, but unfortunately had become weakened and despoiled through internal dissension. A chronic grudge between two of the most prominent members had leavened the whole lump with its unsavory effects. It was one of those situations that afford a pastor a splendid opportunity of losing his ecclesiastical scalp, the very thing that happened to a number of former pastors who undertook to heal the sore. It was not Newgent's policy to take a hand in neighborhood broils, or to break to the woods in the face of such contingencies, but rather to "stand still and see the salvation of the Lord."

His presiding elder told him that his first duty on going to the circuit would be to get the difficulty adjusted. It was suggested that as he was a stranger to both parties, he would be the proper one to do it. He replied that God had not called him to fix up old grudges between church members, but to save sinners.

"But unless you get this done," he was told, "you had as well not go, for you can never accomplish anything until the difficulty is removed. He said he would not bother the old grudge directly, and that if there were sinners who wanted salvation, he was sure God could save them in spite of old, grouchy church members. He proceeded at once to plan a revival campaign. It is part of his philosophy that if a pastor's first revival effort is a success it begets confidence on the part of the people and paves the way for other victories. It is, therefore, the part of wisdom to choose the easiest place to begin with. Accordingly, he began a meeting in the latter part of September at the Rose Hill class, where he thought there were the fewest hindrances. But the people were still busy with their farm work, and with the old trouble still visible around the edges, producing a melancholy Indian summer effect, he had very little encouragement. Two weeks passed and only four persons could be mustered for day services. He preached to this quartet of faithful souls, held prayer and class meetings with them, and encouraged them in every possible way.

"Tell the people to come," he said to his little band one day, as if seized with a sudden revelation, "for we are going to have the biggest revival they have ever seen. If you can't tell it on your own faith, tell them the preacher said so." They perhaps half-way believed what he said. At least they did as they were urged, and the crowd was slightly increased the next day. And with that service the revival really did begin. The prophecy was fulfilled. It was by far the greatest revival the community had ever known, abundantly demonstrating the preacher's philosophy that when folks want salvation, a few backslidden church members, even with their bristles up, cannot prevent them from getting it.

New Goshen Class was the head and heart of the circuit, likewise the seat of the trouble that had been its thorn in the flesh. Newgent proceeded to carry out his policy of capturing the outposts before storming this stronghold of opposition. The plan worked admirably. Three meetings were held, each of which resulted in a sweeping revival. He was now ready for the Herculean task, the final charge, New Goshen itself!

Here it was seen how God moves in mysterious ways, using the weak things to confound the mighty. Some two miles from town lived a family, all of whom were utterly irreligious. The father was a drunkard and a notably rough character. The oldest daughter was an invalid, but on learning of the meeting, she was taken with a keen desire to attend. So she went to visit with a family who lived just across the street from the church, so that it would be convenient for her. In the first service she attended, she went to the altar, and was not there long until she fell into a trance. This was repeated the second and third evenings. One of her brothers was present the third evening, and when he saw his sister so strangely affected, conviction seized upon him so intensely that he likewise fell over in an unconscious condition. When he "came through" he was a new creature in Christ. One after another of this wicked family was taken captive by the power of God until all were graciously saved.

By this time the church began to rub its eyes and take notice. The dry bones were surely beginning to shake and show signs of life. One evening as the power of God was moving upon the people, the two brethren who were responsible for the old trouble on the circuit, were seen edging toward each other, and when they got together, they threw their arms around each other's necks and wept like children. The mother of one of the men was present and when she saw what was taking place, she sent up a shout that really did wake the dead—the spiritually dead of the congregation. Walls of opposition suddenly gave way. The fire from heaven fell as it fell on Sodom and Gomorrah, not to destroy, but to wipe out old scores and to make men and women alive to God. The fortified city was taken. The victory was complete.

During this pastorate of two years, over four hundred persons were added to the church.

One of his most successful and memorable pastorates was that on the Charlestown Circuit, in Illinois. The circuit had a very unsavory reputation at the time. It was commonly known by the undignified and uncomplimentary name of "Dogtown." Newgent had asked to be sent to the worst charge the conference had, and the reputation of Dogtown made this a matter easily determined. His predecessor had been egged and otherwise badly handled.

It was a serious question with the conference as to whether a pastor should be appointed to it, as it had proven itself so unworthy. Besides, it was a proposition that few men were willing to face, Newgent being the only aspirant for the situation. The salary the preceding year was $180, and there was not a church paper taken on the entire charge.

Dogtown, the place which gave the name and largely the reputation to the circuit, was a straggling village noted only for its general cussedness. Newgent declared that it had never been named after a good dog, but more likely after the lowest bred cur in the country. The name, however, was partially a corruption of Diona, by which name the town had been christened; but the appropriateness of the former name was so evident that it naturally stuck, and the original name was well nigh forgotten. Though the place was utterly fallen from righteousness—if it ever possessed any—and was inclined to evil and evil only, it had the one advantage of being well churched. It had two church-houses, each serving as the home for two denominations. Thus, four denominations were diligently casting their pearls into this swine-wallow only to have them trampled under foot. The Methodists and Baptists occupied one house, and the Cumberland Presbyterians and United Brethren the other. They suffered no inconvenience through lack of room, as the combined membership of the four churches numbered only fourteen, seven of whom belonged to the United Brethren.

It was one of those melancholy days, a Sunday afternoon in September, when the new circuit rider arrived to fill his first appointment at Dogtown. Of course the seven members of his flock were present to take his measure. The task was soon done. They were crestfallen when they saw as their spiritual advisor an unpretentious, boyish-looking fellow, somewhat below the standard size, and possessing little of the air and dignity and gravity of a ripe circuit rider, according to their staid notions. The faithful seven, like the proverbial birds of a feather, occupied a portion of the house to themselves; their long faces turned full upon the pastor, added to the melancholy of that autumn afternoon. Nor did the small sprinkling of stray sheep throughout the plain old building serve to any considerable extent as a counter-irritant.

Newgent was keeping a "stiff upper lip" as he introduced the services. The preliminary exercises were about finished, and he was about to begin the sermon; the congregation was droning out a familiar tune when a raw, strapping native came stalking in. He presented a unique appearance. He was barefooted, his trousers were rolled up to his knees, he wore no coat, and his checked shirt was unbuttoned at the collar. No sooner was he seated than another in exactly similar manner and costume followed. One after another followed until upwards in thirty came in, all dressed exactly alike, and so timing their movements as to give time for each to be seated before another followed, making the procession as long as possible—to the amusement of the pastor and the stray sheep, and the utter consternation of the faithful seven.

It struck the witty Irishman at once that they were not trying to install him as the Presbyterians do their pastors, but rather to forestall him after the manner of Dogtown; and he made up his mind not to be forestalled. He was certain they did not want any religion and he had no religion to throw away. He had his subject in mind, but he thought it best to select a more appropriate one. Accordingly, he announced as his text, "Oh, man of God, there is death in the pot." He talked about twenty minutes, putting in the entire time telling his funniest stories, and pouring in one broadside after another of his Irish wit and humor. It was a diplomatic move. All seemed heartily to enjoy the "sermon," except the seven members of his own congregation. The proceeding was most too irregular for their conventional tastes. The members of his uniformed guard were especially delighted. Every witticism was greeted with vociferous applause, by the stamping of their bare feet, clapping of hands, and unrestrained, boisterous laughter.

"I would not black my boots to hear a long, dry sermon," said the preacher by way of conclusion. "You are a fine looking set of fellows. I have been sent by the conference to preach to you, and I am sure we will get along well together. Now, if you see me at any time looking hungry, or if it is near night, take me in. I am an Irishman and easily pleased. And if I see any of you near my home, I will treat you the same. But, gentlemen, I have the most beautiful little wife you ever set eyes on. Now, I expect to bring her with me the next time, and you must be sure to put your boots on and fix up a little."

When he dismissed he went back among this raw element, shaking hands and talking freely with each one. Much of his time between that and the next appointment was spent studying "mischief"—loading up for the next discharge. His second talk was even more humorous than the first, having been prepared especially for the crowd and the occasion. In the meantime his fame had been spread broadcast, and an immense crowd was present to see and hear the "wild Irishman." A number were congregated at the door for the purpose of greeting him upon his arrival at the church.

At the third appointment he had an overflow crowd. As he was walking down the aisle to the pulpit, a brother whom he recognized as one of the true and blue seven of the first service, plucked him aside and whispered:

"Parson, you've got 'em. You're the smartest feller that ever struck this place. These fellers say you've got to have order if they have to fight for it."

"That's what I've been fishing for," said Newgent. He began a revival at this time. Ere long the great, rough fellows who laughed so heartily at his jokes were crowding to the mourner's bench, shedding tears of penitence, crying for mercy, and piercing the air with shouts of victory as one after another emerged into the light and liberty of God's children. A marvelous work was wrought in that sin-polluted community. As the lives of these hardy backwoodsmen were transformed by the power of Christ, they became as potent for righteousness as they had been for evil. Just how many were converted could not be definitely ascertained. One hundred sixty-one members were added to the United Brethren Church, besides those that joined the other churches of the town.

There was an appointment some few miles from Dogtown named Liberty. It was practically dead as a church, there being but five names on the roll, and they represented very little in spiritual assets. He began a revival campaign here immediately following the meeting in town, which proved even more far-reaching in its results. He has always regarded it as the most remarkable revival in his entire ministry. The power of God in the conviction of sinners was irresistible. Strong men and women were stricken unconscious in almost every service. As many as fifty persons could be counted lying in an unconscious condition at one time.

A peculiar feature of this revival was the presence of that strange, nervous phenomenon among the people, known as the "jerks." This strange manifestation prevailed in many of the early revivals where unusual power was displayed. It was especially prevalent in what is known as the great Cumberland revival which swept over the eastern part of Kentucky and Tennessee. Whatever the explanation of this phenomenon, it usually accompanied a deep emotional state, saints and sinners alike being subject to it. The mystery of it and the fact that it often became quite violent, especially on persons who resisted the influence of the meetings, gave it much weight in these early revivals. Peter Cartwright, in his well-known autobiography, describes the physical effects of the jerks as follows:

"No matter whether they were saints or sinners, they would be taken under a warm song or sermon, and seized with a convulsive jerking all over, which they could not by any possibility avoid, and the more they resisted, the more they jerked. If they would not strive against it and would pray in good earnest, the jerking would usually abate. I have seen more than five hundred persons jerking at one time in any large congregation. Most usually persons taken with the jerks, to obtain relief, would rise up and dance. Some would run but could not get away. Some would resist; on such the jerks were usually very severe."

The meeting was accompanied by a variety of spiritual demonstrations, remarkable both in their character and extent. It was entirely beyond human control. It continued four months, day and night. Most of the time there was no preaching, for there was no opportunity for a sermon, and none was needed. The people would gather, singing and shouting as they came, and the singing, shouting, and praying would continue spontaneously. Penitents would go to the altar without an invitation, often as soon as they arrived.

The entire community was charged with a peculiar spiritual atmosphere, the limit of which seemed distinctly drawn. It was termed the "dead line." On reaching this line the individual, whether a Christian or not, would at once be seized with intense religious emotion. On passing out of this region the change was as distinctly felt as on entering it.

So great was the interest in the surrounding country that six schools were closed. One teacher sent to the church for help. Some brethren went to see what was the matter, and found the entire school practically prostrate with conviction. School was turned into prayer meeting. A number, including the teacher, were converted, and school was indefinitely suspended.

The pulpit and platform were smashed into kindling wood at one of the services. People performed physical feats utterly impossible under ordinary circumstances, such as walking across the house on the backs of the pews with their faces turned straight upward. Late one night after the service had closed, a family in the neighborhood heard singing in the direction of the church. Not knowing what it meant, they investigated. But on approaching the church they noticed that the singing was overhead as if produced by an invisible choir in the upper air.

Whatever question may enter the mind as to the nature of these phenomena, there is no question as to the genuineness of the work of grace wrought in that section of country. It was swept as completely by the revival as a prairie is swept by fire. And the effects were abiding, even the more extraordinary forms of spiritual fervor continuing indefinitely.

This was a season of strenuous physical activity on the part of Rev. Mr. Newgent. This meeting lasted four months, and for three months in addition he was in revival meetings continuously.

From being the worst circuit in the conference, Dogtown suddenly became the best. It reported the largest salary. And that year it led the entire denomination in the number of church papers taken. Prizes were offered by the publisher for the largest club in any conference, and also a sweepstakes prize for the largest club in the Church. Newgent won both the conference and the sweepstakes prize, which was the more remarkable when we recall that there was not a paper taken on the charge when he was appointed to it.

Near the close of his memorable meeting at Dogtown, he announced that he would take a missionary offering the following Sunday, and urged the people to come prepared. The missionary meeting was full of enthusiasm, as all his meetings were when a collection was involved. As he was exhorting the congregation to give freely to send the gospel to the heathen, the door opened and a boy bearing in his arms a large rooster came walking down the aisle. As an evidence that the old-time Dogtown spirit was not wholly dead, some mischievous fellows planned to have some fun at the preacher's expense by putting a rooster in the missionary collection. The bird was not only large, but also quite game, and was almost too much for the lad who was to do the presentation act in behalf of the gang. As he proceeded toward the pulpit, his courage began to fail and he hesitated, possibly waiting to see what sort of effect he was producing. The preacher took in the situation at a glance.

"Come on," he said to the half-frightened lad, "I'm the fellow who likes chicken."

With this encouragement the boy went forward and placed his gift in the hands of the preacher, who received it smilingly and thanked him for his generous contribution to the missionary cause. He asked one of the brethren in the "amen corner" to care for his charge while he finished the service. He kept the rooster until fall and took it to the annual conference. In presenting his report, he related the incident and asked in a jocular vein what should be done with the rooster. A dignified, sober-minded brother moved that the rooster be sold and the proceeds be reported to the missionary fund, and that the undignified proceedings be closed. The motion carried.

"All right," said the wiley Irishman, assuming the pose of an auctioneer, "how much am I offered for the rooster? How much do I hear? How much?" Some one ventured a bid. "Sold," said the preacher-auctioneer amid a roar of laughter, and the conference proceeded to more serious matters.

A Unique Missionary Offering.

It was on this charge that he had his first debate. His popularity and success in winning converts led to a challenge from a brother in the Christian (Disciples) church, who was then serving as pastor at Charlestown, Illinois. The question discussed was the divinity of Christ. Newgent took the positive position, affirming that "Christ is the very and eternal God apart from his human nature." The debate was held at Salisbury, Illinois, creating a great deal of interest and attracting a large crowd. That the contest resulted in an easy victory for our subject was attested by the fact that he received an offer from the elders of his opponent's church of fifteen hundred dollars a year to become their pastor, which, at that time, was considered an enormous sum.

"I would not preach your doctrine for fifteen hundred dollars a year," he said, "to say nothing of losing my time and self-respect."

"We are not asking you to preach the doctrine," they said, "all we ask is that you become our pastor; you are at liberty to preach your own convictions." But he was not on the market.

Another interesting experience during this pastorate came as the sequel to a horse trade. One of his neighbors, a brother in the Church, coveted his fine driving horse, and bantered him for a trade. "I have the very horse you need," he urged, and offered what seemed to be a fair bargain. And after the usual ceremonies and preliminaries, the deal was pulled off.

The next day being Sunday, the pastor hitched up his new horse early, and taking his wife and babe, started for his appointment. The animal soon showed signs of treachery, arousing the suspicions of its owner, but they went on. They got on quite well until they came to a low swale in the road over which the water stood several inches deep. When they were about half-way across, the horse stopped and looked back to see if they were coming. But they had also stopped. Newgent, who had some knowledge of "horseology," saw that they were in for it. It being a warm, summer day, an innumerable multitude of mosquitoes soon collected to express their sympathy and to divert the attention of the unfortunate family from their troubles.

"Here's a chance to show that we can keep sweet," said the preacher to his wife, "even under trying circumstances."

The circumstances were indeed trying, for he spent a couple of hours trying to argue the horse out of his position, but the horse was not open to conviction. At the same time he was making a desperate effort to keep sweet, which, with the mosquitoes diligently plying their trade—as it was too good a business opportunity for them to let pass—and the hour for the morning service passing, was not as easy a task as it would have been under less trying circumstances.

"Well," he finally said to his wife, sweetly, "we are going out of here."

"When?" was her meek reply.

"Just as soon as possible." And removing his boots and some other parts of wearing apparel that could be temporarily dispensed with, he got out of the buggy and carried the baby to a dry place. He then removed his wife to the shore, after which he proceeded to unhitch the horse from the buggy, or rather to unhitch the buggy from the horse, as the buggy was movable and the horse was not. A strategic plan was then inaugurated by making a natural appeal to the animal's stubbornness. This was done by hitching the horse to the rear axle-tree of the buggy, which proved a decided success, at least to the extent of getting both the horse and buggy out of the water. Newgent then hitched up according to the conventional style, and with his family started homeward in deep meditation. He filled no appointment that day. He found it difficult to see the point in his neighbor's argument that "this was the very horse he needed," unless it was to stimulate the grace of patience, which is a much-needed quality in a preacher. Since then he has stoutly maintained that it is a bad thing for a preacher to swap horses—unless he is sure he can make a better trade.

CHAPTER NINE.

Labors at Mattoon, Illinois—A Persistent Campaign and a Great Victory—Second New Goshen Pastorate—A Coincidence—Success at Prairieton—Laboring in the Shadow—The Death of Mrs. Newgent—A Bishop's Tribute to her Character.

The scene of his next labors was Mattoon, Illinois. This was a city of some ten thousand inhabitants. It had been marked by a mushroom growth, having sprung from a small village within a few years. More attention, however, had been given to its material development than to its moral and religious welfare. It had eleven churches, but what members they had, were received mostly by letter. Like the city itself, the churches were made up of a conglomeration of heterogeneous elements. All were lacking in efficient organization, stability, and vital godliness.

Rev. Mr. Newgent's church, the United Brethren, like most of the others, was new in the city. It had but twelve members when he took charge. He at once conceived the idea of enlisting the various churches in a great and much-needed revival campaign. He met the local pastors and proposed that all join in a concerted, evangelistic effort—each to begin a meeting in his own church on the same date and continue until victory was achieved. The plan was unanimously agreed to, and on New Year's Day the campaign began.

It was a stubborn fight. The bombardment was kept up by all the churches through the entire month of January with no apparent results. One after another of the pastors then became discouraged and hauled down his colors. By the end of February all the batteries had ceased except two, one of them being Newgent's. Some of his members, convinced of the utter futility of the effort, counseled him to quit. But he was determined to fight it out on that line if it took all summer; and it looked as though it might take several summers. The largest congregation he had during those two months numbered twenty-four.

With the beginning of the third month there were unmistakable evidences of a thaw. Interest was awakened, congregations increased, and on the fifth day of March the ice gave way completely. At the morning service the altar was crowded with anxious penitents, and twenty-one were graciously converted. The news was heralded throughout the city. It was as though a mighty miracle had been wrought. Newgent's church became the center of intense interest, the subject of conversation in the stores and shops and on the streets. At night it seemed as if all Mattoon was seized with a sudden impulse to go to church. The house was filled long before the appointed hour for worship, and the sexton reported that over five hundred people were turned away.

The few days following witnessed stirring scenes in that church. Multitudes were converted; no definite account could be taken of their number. One hundred and twenty-eight members were added to the United Brethren Church, and other churches of the city profited largely from the fruits of the meeting. It was the first genuine revival Mattoon had ever enjoyed.

"What I lacked in sense, I made up in holding on," was Rev. Mr. Newgent's modest comment on the situation. But in this case holding on was only in keeping with his usual good judgment. It was a case where not only prayer and fasting, but also perseverance were required. Perseverance, however, is one of his strong points. As a pastor he made it a rule to continue a meeting until success was realized, a rule that seldom had to be waived.

His labors at Mattoon were followed by a pastorate of two years on the New Goshen charge, making, with a former pastorate of the same length, an aggregate of four years of pastoral services on this field. During these four years he received over six hundred members into the Church and built two church-houses. His work here was also made memorable by what might be termed his first great debate, the details of which are reserved for the next chapter.

The year following was a dark year in his experience, made so by the failure of his wife's health, which resulted in her death. He was serving the Prairieton charge, a charge he had served some years before. His labors here were attended by the usual success—gracious revivals, increased spiritual life and activity, churches thrilled with new zeal and power. A coincidence worth noting in this connection is that his two terms of service on this field resulted in an equal number of accessions to the Church, 203 in each case. "I do not think," he quaintly remarked concerning his second pastorate, "that these were the same 203 that I received when I was there before." The sorry experiences of many pastors with vacillating church members occasioned and justified the remark.

A great meeting at Prairieton stirred up the congregation and led to the rebuilding of their church. It was, however, a great struggle. The church was not strong financially, and the task almost overtaxed their resources. Rev. Mr. Newgent labored unceasingly to pull the enterprise through to a successful consummation, contributing of his own scanty means over three hundred dollars, which necessitated the selling of some of his household goods.

And now, to add to his already heavy burdens, came that which for some time had been recognized as inevitable, and under the deep shadow of which he had been laboring with a heavy heart—the death of his companion. "Kitty" Newgent, as she was affectionately called by her husband and intimate friends, was never strong in body, and for many months she had lingered near the land of shadows. On the day set for the dedication of the church, for the success of which they both prayed and toiled and struggled so heroically, she passed triumphantly to her heavenly home. "Her sun went down while it was yet day."

She died about eight o'clock in the morning. Bishop Jonathan Weaver, who had been secured to dedicate the church, was on the ground for that purpose. When it was learned that the pastor's wife had passed away, the Bishop and members of the church suggested that the dedicatory services be postponed. But as she had helped to plan the day's program, and was so anxious for the success of the occasion, Rev. Mr. Newgent urged that the plans be carried out. So the program of the day was carried out tenderly and lovingly, the church set apart to the worship of Almighty God, while he and his three motherless little ones remained in their sad home by the silent form of the precious wife and mother. Bishop Weaver remained to conduct her funeral. The following account and worthy tribute from his gifted pen was published at the time in the *Religious Telescope*, the official organ of the United Brethren Church:

"Some time ago I arranged with Brother Newgent of the Prairieton Circuit, Lower Wabash Conference, to attend the dedication of a church on his field of labor. Accordingly I left home on Saturday, June 13, and reached Prairieton late in the evening. Upon my arrival there I learned that Brother Newgent's wife was very ill; yet I supposed she might recover. Sunday morning the bell tolled and I knew that some one had passed away. I immediately started for Brother Newgent's home, and on reaching it learned that his wife had just died. It was, indeed, a sad sight. For seventeen years they had shared the sacrifices and trials incident to the life of an itinerant. Now he was left with the care of three little children to fight the battles of life alone. Brother Newgent, as he is wont to do, labored hard to get the church in readiness for dedication, anticipating a good time. But it was a sad day. We attended to the service and dedicated the church with feelings of deep sympathy for the pastor, who, with his little ones, sat beside the earthly remains of a beloved wife.

"Sister Newgent was a patient, kind-hearted Christian woman. She had been in delicate health for a number of years, but neither murmured nor complained. And when the end came, she quietly fell asleep in Jesus. On account of her delicate health, Brother Newgent, for a number of years, seldom remained away from home over night. He would fill his appointment and ride home after services. But no matter how late at night he would return, he would always find a light burning, and usually she would sit up until he returned. But the light is gone out—no, it is burning still. 'There's a light in the window for thee, brother.'"

CHAPTER TEN.

First Great Debate—The Debate as an Institution—The Challenge—Opponents get Weak-Kneed, Prolonging Maneuvers—A Hungry Multitude Unfed—Battle Begins—Questions Discussed—An Improvised Creed for his Opponent—A Premature Baptism—An Opponent's Tribute to his Genius—Crowning the Victor.

In the earlier days of the church great stress was laid upon matters of doctrine. Mooted theological questions occasioned much controversy among the "brethren." Preachers gave special attention to the particular tenets of their respective churches, often decrying with heavy hearts the doctrinal shortcomings of sister denominations. While this was a fault of the times which a broader Christian spirit is overcoming, yet it had its compensating features. In an age of controversy it became every man to have some knowledge, not only of his own church, but also of other churches. It is a fact that people generally were better informed on doctrinal lines than in these latter days when the church is swinging so near the opposite extreme. The doctrinal sermon was then the order of the day, while now it is the rare exception.

The public debate was a popular means of testing the merits of rival religious systems, though in reality it was more a test of the men engaged than of their theology. Nor was the debate confined to matters religious. Its field was unlimited. In politics it was a favorite method of testing political issues and leaders, and of spreading political information. The great Lincoln-Douglas debate is a notable instance. Hence, while it has lost prestige somewhat, the debate once was an honorable and powerful institution. The victor in such a contest was regarded much as the ancient Greeks regarded the winners in the Olympian games. And he was greatly in demand to defend the doctrines of his church against their adversaries. Every pastor needed to cultivate the debating faculty to some extent, at least, for self-protection, just as it was necessary for the early New Englanders to carry their guns with them to church.

It was during Rev. Mr. Newgent's second pastorate at New Goshen that he had his first great debate, and was thrust by force of circumstances into the debating arena. Among his numerous converts were a large number who held the faith enunciated by the Rev. Alexander Campbell, and commonly designated as "Campbellites." This stirred the controversial fires, and in consequence he received a challenge from members of that body to debate publicly certain questions on which the two churches were, perhaps, more content to differ than to agree.

He was quite content to promulgate his faith in the ordinary way, feeling that the results of his work were sufficient proof of the genuineness of his theology. Hence, he sought to avoid being pressed into this sort of contest, even proposing to secure a man to represent his church. But they regarded him as the high priest of his profession, and as they had suffered at his hands, they demanded that he represent his side in person. Seeing there was no honorable way of escape, he reluctantly consented, and preliminaries were arranged.

His opponent was a Rev. Mr. Price. The place selected was a beautiful grove near the village of West Liberty, Vigo County, Indiana. A vast throng of people were present the day the debate was to open. But they were doomed to disappointment. Just as they were getting ready to begin, representatives from the opposition approached Rev. Mr. Newgent and asked if they might be permitted to let the Rev. William Holt, D.D., champion their side instead of Mr. Price. Doctor Holt was a recognized giant among the Campbellites. He was a veteran of thirty-two battles in the debating field, and was one of the foremost expounders of the tenets of his church.

Whether or not it was the wish of Mr. Price to be relieved, it was quite evident that there was a lack of confidence somewhere. At any rate the opposition felt more secure with their cause committed to the hands of their great captain, armed, as he was, with education and eloquence, and skilled in the art and science of debate. All felt that it was to be a great contest, significant in its results, and that no chances should be taken.

Rev. Mr. Newgent consented to the change on condition that the debate be postponed a couple of months to afford time for further preparation. The condition was accepted, and the multitudes were sent away hungry, disappointed, and dejected. The responsibility was thrown upon the Campbellites, as their unwillingness to let Mr. Price champion their side was the cause of the postponement. For the Irish circuit rider it was a diplomatic stroke, a bloodless victory to begin with.

The two months were well spent by Rev. Mr. Newgent in preparation for this greater contest. The delay only seemed to increase popular interest in the affair; and when they again met, the crowd was even larger than before. The discussions consumed eleven days. However, the time was divided into two sections with an intervening period of four or five weeks. It was estimated that from eight thousand to ten thousand people attended daily throughout, among them being a large number of ministers of various denominations. Six boarding tents did a thriving business. In fact, the debate was the great event of the year. A political campaign could not have created more interest and excitement.

The discussions covered six propositions, as follows:

1. The church of which I, William Holt, am a member, is identical in doctrine and practice with the Church of Christ, as revealed in the Scriptures. Holt affirmed.

2. Jesus Christ is the very and eternal God, separate and apart from his human nature. Newgent affirmed.

3. Water baptism is for the remission of the past sins of the penitent believer. Holt affirmed.

4. The Holy Spirit bears a direct, immediate, and personal testimony to the believer of his pardon. Newgent affirmed.

5. Immersion is the only act of Christian baptism. Holt affirmed.

6. After a person is sufficiently instructed in the written Word, the Holy Spirit operates directly upon the heart in regeneration. Newgent affirmed.

In most respects the two men were well matched. Holt was a man of scholarship, a deep, logical thinker, and possessed oratorical ability of a high order, which, with the practice afforded by thirty-two debating bouts, rendered him an antagonist not to be despised. Newgent, then in his prime, possessed a splendid physique, a strong, musical voice that seemed never to tire, which was especially adapted for out-door speaking. Though not a product of the schools, as was his opponent, his mind was strong, clear, and alert. He was ever a close student, not only of books, but of human nature. He could readily analyze a proposition as much by intuition as by logic, and discern at a glance the weak places in his opponent's position. His wit and humor served him well in such matters. When he turned the shafts of ridicule upon a weak point in the position of an opponent, it was as though all the batteries, field pieces, grape and canister, and every other instrument of destructive warfare had been turned loose at once. As there were none of the scholastic or bookish elements in his style, he invariably had the sympathy of the masses.

Doctor Holt made the opening address, affirming that his was the only true church—"identical in doctrine and practice with the Church of Christ as revealed in the Scriptures." He referred to various doctrines held by his church and supported them by Scriptural authority. In most cases they were doctrines accepted by all evangelical churches, affording no ground for controversy. The address was eloquent and logical.

When Newgent arose to reply, he complimented the brother's address and expressed his approval of much that was said. "But now, Mr. Moderator," he continued, "I would like to know what church my brother belongs to when he asserts that they believe thus and so. He frequently referred to 'My church.' If he belongs to a church, how are we to know, in the absence of a written creed, what the doctrines of his church are? Shall we take his statements? That would not be safe, for I find that they differ among themselves on various important points.

"According to Mr. Webster, he has no church. Webster says, 'The Church of Christ is the universal body of Christ.' Paul speaks of the 'whole family in heaven and earth.' All saints in heaven and on earth belong to the Church of Christ. This includes the children. When the disciples asked Jesus who was greatest in the kingdom of heaven, he 'called a little child unto him and set him in the midst of them, and said, Verily, I say unto you, except ye be converted and become as little children, ye shall not enter into the kingdom of heaven.'

"Hence, his church is not THE Church of Christ, neither is it A church of Christ. Again, according to Webster, 'A church of Christ is a body of Christian believers, observing the same rites and acknowledging the same ecclesiastical authority.' It denies all creeds and all ecclesiastical authority. Hence, it cannot be A church of Christ."

He then appealed to the president, urging that, in the absence of a written creed, they should take the writings of their recognized church leaders to ascertain what the doctrines of his opponent's church—granting that it was a church—were. The president so ruled. It then became the duty of Doctor Holt to show that the doctrines indicated were the doctrines of his church according to the church authorities, and also that they were Scripturally sound; and furthermore to prove that other doctrines promulgated by the church leaders, which he had not mentioned, were in strict harmony with the Word.

This opened up a bigger field than even the great high priest of Campbellism was prepared to occupy. Newgent was as familiar with the teachings of his opponent's church as Doctor Holt was himself, and had foreseen and prepared for this emergency.

"I knew you would not be prepared for this, so I thought I would be good to you," he said in a manner suggesting a cat's habit of playing with a mouse just before crushing its bones, "I have, therefore, prepared a creed from the writings of Mr. Campbell and other leaders of your church, which will enable us to ascertain what your church teaches."

He then read the following improvised creed, the different items of which were based upon statements cited in the writings of recognized authorities of the church Doctor Holt was so zealously defending:

I. We profess before all men that we believe in water baptism by immersion; that it is the great panacea for all spiritual maladies.

II. Immersion is the line between the saved and the lost.

III. Immersion is regeneration, conversion, and the new birth.

IV. Immersion is obeying the gospel; it alone is the act of turning to God.

V. Repentance, pardon, justification, sanctification, reconciliation, adoption, salvation, a good conscience, a pure heart, love to God, saving faith, acceptable prayer, the reception of the Holy Spirit, and the intercession of Christ for us, all depend upon immersion.

VI. Immersion is the converting act, and is the most important of all the commandments.

VII. The water is the mother of all Christians.

VIII. We further believe that the Apostles set up the kingdom of Christ on the Day of Pentecost.

IX. That the gospel was first preached by Peter, that the first Christian baptism was administered, and that the reign of grace began on the Day of Pentecost.

X. That the kingdom of Christ has apostatized and become totally corrupt.

XI. That the meaning of the Christian institutions was lost in the Dark Ages, and that no one pleaded the true cause of Christ from the great apostasy until Mr. Campbell's day.

XII. That the true foundation of the millennial church was lost, and that it was laid again in the present century.

XIII. That we have restored the ancient gospel.

XIV. That Mr. Campbell, with others, has from nothing reorganized and established the kingdom of Christ on earth.

XV. That salvation is alone in the society to which we belong, and which was established in the present century.

XVI. We believe in a reformation produced without the Holy Spirit, without godly sorrow, or mourning, or prayer, or any act of devotion whatever.

XVII. That a mere persuasion that the gospel is true is all the faith required.

XVIII. That even a believer is not pardoned, born of God, or in possession of spiritual life until after immersion.

XIX. That no sinner has a right to pray before immersion.

XX. That in regeneration there is no change of the moral powers or inward evidence of the same.

XXI. That sinners are buried in the water in order to kill them to sin.

XXII. That salvation is by works.

XXIII. We deny the divine call to the work of the ministry.

The foregoing propositions had been carefully selected with proof statements by Rev. Mr. Newgent. To square them by the Word of God was a task that even a greater than Doctor Holt might well have shrunk from. And the opening battle which was to decide the question as to whether or not the church of Doctor Holt's choice was identical in doctrine and practice with the New Testament church resulted in a decided advantage in favor of the Irishman.

Among the amusing incidents connected with the occasion was an attempt on the part of the Holt allies to create a demonstration favorable to their cause. On the day when the subject of baptism was up, a rumor came to Newgent's ears that a pretended convert to his opponent's doctrine would present himself for admission to the Campbellite Church at the evening service. A baptismal service would then be held the following morning in a nearby creek in the presence of the crowd, affording ocular evidence that the champion of immersion was gaining ground. This, attended with all the pomp and display necessary to make it impressive, it was expected, would prove a staggering blow to Newgent, from which even his wit and humor would not enable him to rally.

He did not give much credence to the rumor, scarcely believing that any one would resort to such tactics, but thought it best to keep at least one eye open. The evening services were held in the churches, both denominations being represented in the village. Each church would have preaching by a visiting minister of its own faith. Ordinarily those who cared to attend would go to their own church, the champions themselves remaining at home to rest and gird themselves for the next day. Newgent, however, curious to learn whether there was any foundation for the rumor, on that particular evening attended the service at his opponent's church. To his surprise, he saw Doctor Holt there. He then smelled a rat. At the close of the sermon, Doctor Holt arose, delivered a brief exhortation and opened the doors of the church. And the rat smelled stronger.

All doubts were dispelled when an old, rusty-looking gentleman limped forward and gave the preacher his hand. This was the convert that the eloquence of Doctor Holt had won to the standard of Campbellism—an old, decrepit man, by no means distinguished for learning or intelligence, who had been imported from an adjoining county for the occasion!

REV. ANDREW JACKSON NEWGENT

At age of forty.

The doctor was, of course, glad that one penitent was making the "good confession," and announced that on to-morrow morning at eight o'clock, just before the day's exercises would begin, they would repair to the creek and "baptize the brother into Christ."

At this juncture Rev. Mr. Newgent arose and asked if he might say a few words. The permission was granted. "Doctor," he said, "I have been taking it for granted that you were sincere in advocating that the penitent's sins were pardoned only in the act of baptism. Now, here is a dear brother desiring to flee the wrath to come. Suppose he should die before eight o'clock to-morrow morning, and thus be lost. Who would be responsible? He is getting old. Aren't you running an awful risk in exposing his soul to eternal death until to-morrow? Doctor, don't you think it would be safer and more consistent to take this brother at once to the creek and baptize him into Christ?"

The doctor admitted that he was right, and ordered the candidate to be baptized immediately. A small bodyguard took him to the creek and reluctantly performed the task. Thus evaporated the scheme from which the opposition had hoped to reap so largely. They did reap largely, but not what they expected. In his opening remarks the next morning, Newgent recited with dramatic effect the story of the exploded plot, taking ample time to do it justice. The story was told with many a humorous and oratorical flourish, producing roar after roar of laughter from the great audience. The house thus built upon the sand fell upon the heads of the unwise builders with most disastrous effect.

As an illustration of his peculiar power over the minds of his hearers, the following tribute from a titled minister of the Campbell faith will serve well. He was taking his usual rest during the noon intermission, when the reverend gentleman who wore a D.D. and a silk hat, approached him, and after introducing himself, said:

"Rev. Mr. Newgent, they have told me that you attended school but three months in your life, and also that this is your first debate. I am convinced that in this you have been misrepresented. I heard Doctor Holt deliver his opening address to-day, and I thought no man on earth could answer his argument. But when you got up to speak, you had not proceeded five minutes until the people had forgotten all he had said. The same was true of the second address, and I saw at once that our man was beaten."

Newgent told him that he had had but meager school advantages. In a former chapter it is stated that he attended school three terms of three months each. But as school attendance then was very irregular at the best, the gentleman's information was not far from the truth. He informed his friend, however, that he had always been a hard student, and thus had atoned in some measure for the meagerness of his school advantages.

"Well," said the doctor of divinity, "I expected to remain until the close of the debate; but I see that our man is fighting a losing battle, and I do not care to stay and see him defeated." And after a few further remarks, he bade Rev. Mr. Newgent a courteous good by and left the grounds, not desiring to see the end of a contest that boded no good thing for his cause.

The gentleman's unwilling prophecy was fulfilled, no doubt, to a larger degree than he himself anticipated. Newgent seemed to gain power and momentum to the last. When the great contest closed, defeat was plainly written upon the countenance of every Holt sympathizer, while Newgent was showered with compliments and congratulations from his admiring friends. A delegation of Baptist brethren, headed by the pastor of the First Baptist Church of Terre Haute, rushed forward and placed a ten-dollar hat on his head in behalf of that denomination. Commendations and substantial tokens of approval came from representatives of a number of denominations. And the occasion ended pleasantly for all, except the number whose theological bias was plainly and painfully indicated by their crestfallen spirits.

CHAPTER ELEVEN.

Subsequent Debates—The Owen Contest—He Gets his "Treat"—Opponent's Confession—Dressing "Stone"—A Scared Baptist—Invades the Lutheran Ranks— Measures Steel with Doctor Ingram—Dissertation on Infant Baptism—Opponent's Early Flight—Concludes the Debate Alone—The Haw Debate.

As the preceding chapter has shown, our subject was not a debater from choice. He was thrust into the debating arena by circumstances. His memorable victory over Doctor Holt placed his name in big letters among the leading debaters of the time, creating demands for his services in this capacity that could not well be resisted. Besides being in constant demand to expound and defend the doctrines for which he stood, by his own, and other denominations of a kindred faith, he figured in some thirteen debating bouts, a detailed account of which would of itself make a good-sized volume. Hence, a few passing references to some of these contests, with some characteristic incidents, is all that will be attempted here.

Shortly after the debate with Doctor Holt, he received an urgent appeal from Rev. James Griffiths of the United Brethren Church at Potomac, Illinois, to come over to his Macedonia and help him. Controversy between the Christian and United Brethren churches of that section was at white heat. The Christian Church, under the leadership of a Rev. Mr. Owen, was pressing the battle to the gates and making things unpleasantly interesting for Rev. Mr. Griffiths, who was not of a controversial turn of mind. He felt, however, that the safety of his cause demanded that his adversaries be met upon their own ground with their own weapons. His presiding elder, Rev. J. W. Nye, joined in the request that Rev. Mr. Newgent go to the rescue.

Accordingly, a debate between Owen and Newgent, covering the usual mooted questions between the two denominations, was arranged. Rev. Mr. Owen was scholarly and serious, but utterly lacking in the humorous element. His dry logic was no match for the fiery eloquence and quick wit of his Irish antagonist. Like the bridegroom at a wedding, he was a rather inconspicuous figure, except that his part was necessary to the carrying out of the program. It was an easy victory for the United Brethren and their allies, resulting in a cessation of hostilities and a reign of peace in that section of Zion.

A more notable contest was that with Dr. W. B. F. Treat, then president of Indiana State University, at Bloomington. Doctor Treat, as his position would indicate, was a man of fine scholarship. He was a minister in the Christian Church, zealous in the defense of its doctrines, and had won many trophies as a debater.

The preliminary arrangements for this debate were made by a couple of ministers, one a representative of the Christian Church, and the other a United Brethren. Newgent and Treat were secured by the two churches as their respective champions.

As the two champions were introduced on the occasion of the debate, the following bit of repartee was indulged in by Newgent, who had been suffering from some slight temporary ailment: "I am sorry you are not in good trim," said Doctor Treat, "I had hoped to find a man who would be able to put up a good fight."

"Oh," said Newgent, "I think I'll feel better when I get my *Treat*."

In his opening remarks, Doctor Treat again indulged in some pleasantry at Newgent's expense. He referred to his opponent as having been born in Green County and cradled in a sugar trough. Newgent replied that he had missed it four miles as to the place of his birth. The sugar trough part of it, however, he did not deny; but as the trough had served well to cradle the different members of his mother's small family of nine children, he was quite sure the rude cradle suffered no violence at his hands.

The learned doctor further tried to discount the scholarship of his opponent by referring to a postal card received from him on which there were two words misspelled. To this Newgent also had an answer. "Great speakers," said he, "are usually deficient in other lines. I now understand why the doctor is short on debating; all his strength has gone into his spelling."

The usual questions were discussed, six in number, the same as in the great Holt debate. The arguments were listened to by thousands of interested and enthusiastic spectators, among them ministers and dignitaries of various denominations, and persons of prominence in educational, political, and professional circles. As to the result of the contest, Doctor Treat's own confession, as brought out in the following incident, will suffice:

A debate between Newgent and a Rev. Dr. J. W. Stone, of St. Louis, Missouri, also a minister of prominence in the Christian Church, was scheduled to take place a few weeks later. In the meantime Doctor Stone, anxious to learn all he could concerning his opponent, sought an interview with Doctor Treat. He met him at a church dedication at which Treat was officiating. The two men, with others, were entertained for dinner at the same home after the morning service. At an opportune time, Doctor Stone introduced the subject in which he was especially interested, and the following conversation between the two men took place, being overheard and reported to Newgent by a gentleman who leaned toward his side of the question:

"Are you acquainted with a United Brethren preacher in Indiana of the name of Newgent?" Doctor Stone inquired.

"I am," was President Treat's answer.

"Did you not debate with him some time ago?"

"I did."

"Is he a scholar?"

"I do not know."

"Is he logical?"

"I cannot tell. He claimed that he went to school only a few months."

"How long did you debate with him?"

"Six days."

"What?" said Doctor Stone in astonishment, "You debated with him six days, and could not tell whether or not he is educated?"

"Well," continued the university president, in a meditative mood, "I will say that he is—*forceful*."

Doctor Stone looked blank for a moment, and then ventured with a smile, "May be he whipped you?"

"I don't know," was the guarded answer, "but I am inclined to believe that my people thought he did." Observing that Stone was intensely interested, Treat inquired:

"Are you thinking of debating with him?"

Stone answered in the affirmative.

"Can't you get out of it in some honorable way?"

Stone replied that he was not wanting "out of it."

"But you may want out of it," was Treat's not very assuring reply.

"Why, is he not fair in debate? Is he not a gentleman?"

"Yes," answered Treat, "so much so that all your people who know him love to be with him and hear him talk." And the conversation drifted into other channels. But Doctor Stone, being from Missouri, waited to be shown. And the debate was held according to schedule.

About this time Doctor Stone was enjoying no small degree of notoriety. He had debated with a Methodist minister in southern Illinois, and so completely mastered him that he acknowledged his defeat in sack cloth and ashes, and joined the Christian Church. Stone was taking advantage of his newly-acquired popularity in waging a relentless war against the "sects," as he termed them, when some of the Pedo-Baptists secured Newgent to meet him in debate. And the challenge was brought to the great, self-important Doctor Stone.

"Newgent!" said this supposed Goliath with a contemptuous sneer. "He can't debate. He's an Irish peddler who used to sell table-cloths in my father's neighborhood." The committee informed him that they were willing to risk their case with the Irish peddler. However, Stone's visit to Doctor Treat to get information concerning the Irishman would indicate that his contempt was more feigned than real.

The debate was held in a small town in southern Illinois, where the doctor had been making havoc of the "sects." The table-cloth story became current, and much speculation was indulged in concerning the supposed vender of household commodities. His coming to the village was awaited with intense interest. When the train on which he was scheduled to arrive pulled in at the station, a curious and enthusiastic crowd was waiting to get a view of the man who dared to dispute the wisdom of Doctor Stone. As he stepped from the car, a gentleman who knew him said, pointing him out, "There's the table-cloth peddler."

A hearty salute was given by the crowd. Newgent, having been apprised of the story, was equal to the occasion. As soon as the hubbub ceased, he addressed the crowd, turning the table-cloth story against his opponent in the following speech:

"Gentlemen, if you have come here to buy table-cloths, you will be disappointed. I have changed my occupation. I have been informed that there is some fine stone in southern Illinois, so I have come down here to set up my shop and spend a few days dressing Stone."

The "Stone dressing" joke superseded the table-cloth story and became a catch phrase throughout the debate.

It is likely that Stone often called to mind the friendly advice of Doctor Treat, and regretted that he did not take it. He could cope neither with the argument, the quick wit, nor the physical endurance of his opponent. His voice failed completely, and the last two addresses of Newgent were unanswered. The Stone-dressing business proved eminently successful.

An amusing incident occurred in connection with a debate in Kentucky with a Doctor Fairchilds, an eminent Baptist minister. A story came to the ears of Doctor Fairchilds after he came on the ground, to the effect that Newgent was a man of extraordinary scholarship, that he was master of some thirteen languages, etc. The doctor was visibly disconcerted by the story, and after hearing Newgent's first address, was fully persuaded that it was true, especially the part relating to the thirteen languages. He was quite nervous, and utterly broke down about the middle of the program, leaving the supposed master of thirteen languages easily master of the situation.

While on his official rounds as superintendent of the Tennessee Mission Conference, he once chanced to invade a Lutheran community, which set in motion a train of influences that terminated in a debate with a representative of that body. This was about eight miles from Greenville. He was visiting a United Brethren family that had moved into the community, and in company with his host, called at the district school, and made a talk to the pupils. Through the influence of his host, the school house was secured for a preaching service that evening. Other influences then began to be felt, and the meeting was continued indefinitely, resulting in a sweeping revival, the organization of a United Brethren church, and the building and dedication of a church-house within two months from the close of the revival.

This occasioned great concern among the Lutherans who lost quite heavily as a result of the United Brethren invasion. To regain their lost ground, they challenged Rev. Mr. Newgent to debate certain doctrinal questions with a representative of their church. Newgent was then in his element, in the debate, and answered that he would be ready at any time to accommodate them.

The Lutheran champion was Dr. J. C. Miller, president of one of their church schools. The much-mooted question as to what body constituted the true church was the first taken up, Doctor Miller posing as the representative of a church whose doctrines and usages are identical with those taught and exemplified in the New Testament.

This placed upon Miller the Herculean task of defending the various tenets and practices peculiar to his church. Among other specimens of Lutheran creed, Newgent read the following: "The infant's heart is corrupt, and it cannot be saved unless baptized by a Lutheran minister with heavenly, gracious water." When asked if his church taught that, Doctor Miller admitted that it did.

Newgent showed this bit of dogma up in a bad light by the use of an object lesson. Borrowing a baby from a mother in the audience, he held it up before the crowd, stating that the "little rascal's" heart is corrupt and its only chance for salvation was by being baptized according to the Lutheran formula. "Now," he continued, "I want this brother to demonstrate to this audience how a baby must be saved. I want him to change this baby's heart from a state of corruption to a state of purity. I want to see how a baby is saved, for, according to his theology, I have three babies in hell."

The brother winced under this outburst of sarcasm. He refused to baptize the child, which, had he done so under the circumstances, would scarcely have made his doctrine appear less obnoxious. Other peculiar Lutheran tenets appeared to the same disadvantage under similar treatment, and the church's hope of gaining its lost ground completely vanished. The debate popularized the United Brethren Church, giving it a strong hold in the community. Flag Branch, a flourishing rural church, stands as a monument to Rev. Mr. Newgent's labors in that section.

Another contest worthy of special note was with a Baptist minister at Blue Springs, Tennessee, in 1882. The mode of baptism was a live question throughout that region. The battle line was drawn by the Baptists and Pedo-Baptists. They finally agreed to have the question discussed in a public debate, each side to furnish its champion. Three churches were represented on the immersion side, and seven on the other. The immersionists secured as their representative, Doctor Ingram, a prominent Baptist divine of Virginia. Newgent was selected by the anti-immersionists. The debate was to cover six propositions and to continue six days, one subject being slated for each day.

The Baptists were very desirous of including infant baptism in the list of subjects to be discussed. This was a question that Newgent had never debated, and in which he had very little interest. But to accommodate the Baptists, he consented to defend the practice of infant baptism. His opponent proposed the question, stating it as follows: "*Resolved*, That infants are fit subjects for baptism." Newgent consented to affirm it.

It was slated for the second day. In his opening remarks, Newgent said: "Mr. President, this is a peculiar question; but my brother wrote it and insisted that I affirm it. It is peculiar from the fact that I am not to prove that the child needs baptism, or that there is any command for infant baptism, or that there ever was an infant baptized. I am simply asked to prove that a child is a fit subject for baptism."

At these remarks a storm of protest arose from the immersionists. They expected him to defend the vast array of teaching that the various Pedo-Baptist bodies had put forward on the subject.

"Keep cool," he said to the immersionist part of the crowd as they were clamoring for a hearing and creating no little confusion. "Doctor Ingram and I signed these papers, and we agreed to be governed by the board of moderators. This question simply deals with the child's fitness for baptism. I appeal to the moderators." The moderators sustained his position.

He then asked his opponent whether or not the Baptist Church would baptize a subject until he was converted and became as a little child. His opponent stated that it would not. This gave him a splendid foundation for his address, and, at the same time, removed the last foundation stone from under his opponent, so far as infant baptism was concerned. He made an earnest and eloquent address, showing that the child is a type of the heavenly citizen, and as such possesses special fitness for all the sacraments of God's house.

While he was talking, his attention was called to Doctor Ingram. The doctor, grip in hand, was making rapid strides toward the railroad station. His moderator and some friends were accompanying him, trying to persuade him to remain. But he could endure it no longer.

The doctor's retreat caused a great sensation, relished immensely by the Pedo-Baptists, but a bitter dose to the immersionists. There were yet four days of the program remaining. Newgent's side demanded, as they were paying him for his work, that he remain and carry out his part of the program. This he did, but as the debate had only one end to it during those four days, it spoiled the excitement, though it served well the purpose of those who had employed him.

Among his later debates was one held in 1898 at Mechanicsville, Indiana. Dr. J. W. Haw, of the Christian Church, was his opponent on this occasion. Doctor Haw had been holding revival meetings in that part of Indiana, and being dogmatic in style and controversially inclined, was unsparing in his denunciations of other denominations. His aggressions and criticisms were disturbing the equilibrium of some of the brethren whose churches were being used as a target by this ecclesiastical Nimrod. They wrote to Newgent, then in Tennessee, urging him to champion their side against Doctor Haw in debate, offering him fifty dollars per day and expenses for his time. He consented on condition that the propositions were fair and that the reverend gentleman in question was a representative man in his church.

He was referred to a two-column article in a current number of the *Christian Standard* relating to Doctor Haw. The article was extravagant in the use of adjectives describing the doctor's ability and achievements, stating that he was the leading debater in the Christian Church, having had more such battles than any other man in it at that time. This was quite satisfactory to Newgent, as at that period he did not care to waste any shot or shell on small game.

In this, as in all other such contests, Newgent abundantly sustained his position and satisfied the expectations of his supporters. His experience, self-control, complete mastery of the subjects in hand, humor, and physical endurance made him an antagonist that even the greatest debater in a debating church could illy cope with. The general verdict of even Doctor Haw's own sympathizers was that it was decidedly a one-sided affair.

CHAPTER TWELVE.

Perrysville and Centerpoint—Industry Rewarded from an Unsuspected Source—A "Slick" Wedding—Fruitful Labors at Centerpoint—A One-Sided Union Meeting—The Doctrine of the Resurrection Again Demonstrated.

A year on the Perrysville charge in the Upper Wabash Conference, followed by a year at Centerpoint, in his own conference, the Lower Wabash, covering 1874 to 1876, closed Rev. Mr. Newgent's work in the pastorate for a season. It was from the latter charge that he received his appointment from the Home, Frontier, and Foreign Missionary Society as Superintendent of the Tennessee Mission Conference. From thenceforth he was destined to serve the Church in a larger capacity, though there is no work that he regards as more exalted or more vital to the progress of the kingdom than that of the pastor. And it is but just to say that there is no work in which he has been happier or more in his element. The pastor, he regards, as the pivotal man in the church militant, around whose personality must revolve all the machinery of its organized life. Hence, in whatever position he has been placed, he has ever been in fullest sympathy with the men on the firing line, and has sought in every way to encourage and magnify their work.

His going to Perrysville was in response to an urgent appeal from his intimate friend, Dr. J. W. Nye, then a popular presiding elder in the Upper Wabash Conference. His work here was fruitful and congenial, and marked by some rich experiences, which he carries with him as refreshing memories. One of these teaches a practical moral lesson, namely, that honest industry has its reward in more ways than one.

It need not be explained here that industry is a part of his religion. He believes with Paul that it does not injure, or lower the dignity of a minister to labor with his hands. In this, as in other respects, he made himself an example to the flock. Odd moments are always occupied in diversions of a practical character. The outward appearance of the parsonage never failed to testify to his thrift and good taste. A garden served as an outlet to his surplus physical energies as well as a means of supplementing the usually modest income. Under his skillful hand it invariably became a thing of beauty and an object of just pride.

Some five miles from Perrysville lived a horny-handed son of the soil, a man who made industry not only the chief element in his religion, but the sum total of it. He was an infidel in his belief—or disbelief—and regarded the church as an imposition, and preachers as an indolent, worthless lot. Passing through the village one day, he noticed Rev. Mr. Newgent's garden. It was by far the finest he had seen. His surprise can only be imagined when, upon inquiry, he learned that the owner of it was one of those lazy preachers.

A few days later he drove up to the parsonage with a barrel of flour, which he unloaded and unceremoniously rolled upon the porch. This time the surprise was on the preacher, as a reputation for benevolence was a thing of which, up to that time, the infidel could not boast. He explained that ordinarily he had no use for preachers, but as he had found one that was not lazy, he "wanted to help him." The donation was an expression of his regard for the minister who showed a willingness, according to the infidel's conception of the term, to earn his bread in the sweat of his face.

Another incident, picked up at random, occurred one cold day during the winter of his stay at Perrysville. A couple whose appearance did not indicate a superabundance of worldly prosperity, came to the parsonage to be married. They had come from the adjoining county, the boundary between the two counties being the Wabash River, on the bank of which Perrysville was located. The river was frozen over. The couple traveled afoot, having crossed the river on the ice. The preacher explained that they would have to recross the river before the ceremony could be performed, as the law required that marriages be solemnized in the county in which the license was issued. So he conducted the matrimonial candidates to the river.

When the preacher was satisfied that they had proceeded beyond the half-way point on the river, he ordered the couple to halt and join hands. By this time their presence had attracted the attention of the young people who were out on the ice in large numbers enjoying the fine winter sport of skating. As the wedding was a public function, no restrictions being placed on attendance, the ceremony was performed in the presence of an enthusiastic multitude.

The service completed, the groom, who was unacquainted with ministerial usages, inquired as to the amount of the fee. To save him the responsibility and further embarrassment of determining the sum to be paid for the service, the preacher suggested that a dollar would be sufficient, fearing lest he might set the price too high for his purse. Even at that it was painfully evident that the young man's financial rating was overestimated. After nervously fumbling through his pockets he was able to produce but fifty cents. In his dilemma he found it necessary to call upon his bride for financial assistance. Happily she was equal to the emergency, and supplied the deficit from her own purse.

The Young Man's Financial Rating Was Over-estimated.

"This is the fairest wedding I have ever seen," said the preacher. "It has always been my opinion that the lady ought to help pay the preacher, and she receives as much benefit from the ceremony as does the man. I hope you will always share each other's burdens in this way." And wishing them happiness and prosperity, he sent them on their way rejoicing.

The local paper gave a flowery account of the wedding that took place on the ice, stating that it was the "slickest" wedding that had ever occurred in that section. But the minister's fee and the manner of paying it was not allowed to become public, lest it should become a troublesome precedent in matrimonial circles.

The following year, which was spent on the Centerpoint charge, was a most fruitful one. Here, as in so many other places, he found a splendid opportunity of demonstrating his favorite doctrine of the resurrection—the resurrection of dead churches. The spiritual life of the churches at Centerpoint was at ebb tide, and had been for an indefinite time. Soon after his arrival the Methodist pastor, who was also new in the town, called upon him to confer as to their plans for revival work. As workers were scarce, it was thought best to plan their meetings so that they would not conflict. Rev. Mr. Newgent, Abraham-like, let his brother do the choosing, and the brother, perhaps as anxious as Lot to get in on the ground floor, decided to commence a revival at once. Newgent began a meeting at the same time some few miles in the country. Newgent's meeting immediately developed into a revival of so great proportions that it became the one overshadowing event of the whole country, drawing the Methodist pastor's congregation from him and rendering it impracticable for him to continue. His situation was a rather lonely one. In his extremity he sought another interview with his fellow pastor, proposing to close his meeting at once if Newgent would join him later in a union revival effort.

This Newgent consented to do on three conditions, as follows:

1. That the meetings be held in the United Brethren church.

2. That the United Brethren pastor do all the preaching.

3. That the United Brethren pastor do the managing.

Hard as the conditions seemed, the brother agreed to them. The conditions, in fact, look egotistical and perhaps selfish on the surface, but when the United Brethren pastor explained his reasons for them they were seen to be neither. On the contrary they were meant for the highest good of both churches, and were abundantly vindicated by the outcome. He was intensely anxious that Centerpoint have a genuine revival of religion. To promote such a revival at any cost was his purpose. That this purpose might be realized he would not permit modesty, formality, or any other creature to stand in the way.

The United Brethren Church was the more commodious and had the advantage in location. This was the reason for the first condition. The reason for the second and third conditions was that Centerpoint had been preached to death. A change of methods was imperative if the people were to be reached. He wanted a meeting without preaching, without too much human agency, but where God himself might control to his own glory. Only by having the management left to him could he apply the remedy needed according to his diagnosis of the case.

His plan was now to be put to the test—a revival without preaching, the laity to do the work as they felt divinely moved. The meeting began on a Friday evening. But with no life there could be no real activity. The chariot wheels dragged heavily at the first. On Sunday morning he announced that at four o'clock p. m., a children's meeting would be held. Aside from selected helpers, only children within a certain age limit would be admitted. Such meetings even at that date were quite uncommon. The announcement, therefore, aroused a great deal of curiosity. But that was one point in the announcement. Something must be done to stir the people. There must be a new avenue of approach to their cold hearts.

The children's service produced the desired effect. At the appointed hour the house was filled to overflowing. There were three helpers, all ministers, present, who did their part according to Newgent's directions. Songs were sung, prayers offered by the ministers as they were called upon, a brief talk by the leader, some simple propositions, and the meeting closed in less than a half-hour from the time it began. But that half-hour turned the tide in Centerpoint. The children became the vanguard in a religious movement that was to shake the town from center to circumference. Many of them went home weeping to speak of the longing of their tender hearts to fathers and mothers, who, in turn, were awakened to a consciousness of their own need.

At the evening service which followed, seventy-five persons came to the altar, most of whom professed conversion. The revival was no longer a problem. It spread throughout the town and community like fire in dry stubble. The church arose from the grave of lethargy and formalism, cast off her grave clothes—and the doctrine of the resurrection was again abundantly demonstrated.

CHAPTER THIRTEEN.

Becomes a Missionary Superintendent—Second Marriage—An Unexpected Welcome—Forms a Quaker Friendship—The Spirit Moves in a Quaker Meeting—A Quaker's Prayer Answered—Builds a College—Shows What to do for a Dead Church—Another Tilt on the Doctrine of Baptism—Conversion of a Dunkard Preacher—Turns a Great Movement in the Right Direction.

In the fall of 1876, Rev. Mr. Newgent entered upon his duties as Superintendent of the Tennessee Mission Conference, under appointment of the Home, Frontier, and Foreign Missionary Association. In the meantime he had married Miss Annie Crowther, of Terre Haute, Indiana, who, under the divine blessing, abides as the companion of his joys and sorrows amid the lengthening shadows. She is a woman of rare and excellent qualities, which especially fitted her for her position as the wife of an active and ambitious minister. She is in fullest accord with her husband's ambitions and tastes, and has contributed her part toward the success of his career. He freely accords to her this credit. With this queenly woman ordering its affairs, the Newgent home has ever been a haven of real rest, a retreat for God's servants especially. It extends a welcome and hospitality—a true home spirit—that at once makes the wayworn pilgrim feel at ease in body and mind, and charms the hearts of the young as well.

At the time of their removal to Tennessee, the United Brethren Church was new in the South. Its attitude of open hostility to slavery largely shut it out of regions south of Mason and Dixon's line. The Tennessee Conference then had less than four hundred members, with only six houses of worship. So a great field spread out before the new Superintendent, taking him back to conditions in many respects similar to those in which he began his ministerial labors. It was still a time of reconstruction in church affairs as well as in matters political. But his was a work of construction rather than of reconstruction.

Aside from the need of laborers and the vast opportunities afforded for building up the church in this section, one reason he had for accepting this appointment was the condition of his own and his wife's health. Both were threatened with failing health, and a change of climate was advised, the high altitude of eastern Tennessee being recommended as especially adapted to their physical needs.

They arrived at Limestone, Tennessee, on a Friday evening in September. Here was illustrated how his fame as a genial, good humored personality had spread throughout the Church, so that the people felt that they were acquainted with "Jack" Newgent (later Uncle Jack) even though they had never met him personally. Arriving at the city some time after dark, worn by the long journey, the discomforts of which were aggravated by their poor health, they little dreamed of finding in that particular realm an acquaintance or anyone who had any concern for them.

Great indeed was Newgent's surprise when, as he alighted from the train, a gentleman, a total stranger, with a lantern on his arm, stepped up and in a familiar manner accosted him, "Hello! Is this Jack Newgent?"

He had been so familiarly known as "Jack," that he had resolved to be known by the more grave and dignified appellation of Andrew J. Newgent when he came into his new kingdom. But his expectation perished, as it would have done even had the circumstances been otherwise. A man's name, like his clothes, is a part of him, and if it does not fit, his friends will persist in trimming it until it does. The personality and the title cannot be unequally yoked together.

"Well," said the reverend gentleman from the Hoosier State, "I suppose if I should land in the heart of Africa, some Hottentot would come rushing out of the jungle and say, 'Hello, Jack Newgent!' Who are you, anyway?" The stranger was Mr. W. C. Keezel, a prominent layman in the conference, who had been advised of their coming by Dr. D. K. Flickinger, Secretary of the Missionary Society, and was there to take them to his hospitable home. It was a pleasant surprise, and they felt at once that they were among friends whose hearts God had touched with his spirit of kindness and tenderness. Their anxieties were dispelled, and they felt as near heaven in Tennessee as in Indiana.

Next day his host took him on a ten-mile ride by horseback over a mountain road to a quarterly conference, where he met a number of ministers, and began to get acquainted with his new co-workers. His presence filled the little band of faithful toilers with new hope and courage. He preached the following day (Sunday) at a neighboring church to an immense crowd. Here he met Rev. Eli Marshall, a minister of repute in the Quaker—or Friends—church, with whom he was destined to form a close friendship, a friendship which revealed later to both of these servants of God how mysteriously God moves in answer to the earnest prayers of his faithful children.

Rev. Mr. Marshall was not only an able minister, but was also a successful business man, being the owner of several plantations. He took Newgent to his home, and later showed him a congenial cottage on one of his plantations. "This is at thy disposal," he said, "if it suits thee." Newgent replied that it was just such a place as he was looking for, as it was but a short distance from town and the railroad station, and inquired as to the rental value.

"Just move in," said Marshall, "we will talk about that some other time."

But when Newgent insisted, he set a nominal price, which indicated that he was not especially concerned about the financial side of the transaction. He furthermore insisted on transporting Newgent's household goods from the station, but this privilege he was compelled to share with Mr. Keezel. While they were moving his goods from the train, his Quaker neighbors set to work and filled the smoke-house with provisions, and supplied sufficient fuel to last him through the winter. Such expressions of kindness and generosity seldom had been seen.

The fourth week in October was the time for the Quakers' yearly meeting, to be held at Rev. Mr. Marshall's home church. He had issued an order to Newgent to have no engagement for that time, as his presence and help were desired at the meeting. Under the circumstances there was but one thing to do, and that was to respect the order. These meetings were matters of no small significance in that denomination. They usually lasted several days, and were great seasons of fellowship. They were very largely attended so that the program sometimes had to be carried out in several sections. Newgent had never had the privilege of attending a Quaker meeting, but his appreciation of the Quakers by this time knew no bounds.

He first went to the meeting on Saturday morning and was surprised to find more than a thousand people on the ground. His friend, Rev. Mr. Marshall, met him immediately and said, "If the Spirit moves thee to preach to-day, we want thee to preach in the church this morning." Some one was to preach in the school house nearby. The Spirit moved, and Newgent preached.

In the afternoon he was "moved" to preach again. He was urged to preach again at night. This time the Spirit was not consulted, but his preaching had touched a responsive chord in the Quaker heart, so it was taken for granted that the Spirit would be favorable. An out-door service and a service in the school house besides that in the church were required in order to accommodate the crowd. Newgent declined to preach at this time, not wishing to usurp the honors that belonged to the Quaker preachers. But the Quaker "Spirit" refused to let him off. He was even urged to sing a special song, which was a great departure from Quaker usage in those days. While preaching with his usual power, it was evident to him that great conviction prevailed in the congregation. As he had been invited to depart from one of the Quaker usages, he now felt bold to depart from another. Indeed he felt strongly moved by the Spirit to give an invitation for seekers to come to the altar. The invitation given, the altar was soon crowded with anxious penitents. He then called upon the Quakers to come forward and to sing and pray with the seekers. This a considerable number did, casting aside all reserve, and the meeting became a typical United Brethren revival. It was one time when the Spirit "moved" beyond question in a Quaker meeting.

He was given right of way in the church on Sunday morning, Sunday evening, and Monday evening. A new element was thus diffused into Quakerdom. He held a meeting in that same community a few weeks later, in which the Quakers took a leading part, and which resulted in about a hundred conversions.

The best part of the whole procedure came to light when Newgent called to pay his landlord the small pittance that was due on rent. Rev. Mr. Marshall refused to accept even the nominal amount that had been agreed upon.

"Let me explain," he said, "I have never told anybody what I am going to tell thee—not even my wife. Some three months ago I moved my foreman out of that house, and began to pray for the Lord to send us a good, live preacher from the North. I had got tired of these slow-going Southern fellows. But I forgot to tell the Lord to send a Quaker. So the Lord was free to send whomsoever he pleased. And the first time I heard thee preach, I said, 'There is the answer to my prayer.' Now, it would not do for me to charge rent of the man the Lord sent in answer to my prayer, when he is living in the property I vacated for him when I besought the Lord to send him. That house is for thee as long as thee wants it."

When this noble soul was called to heaven some years later, Rev. Mr. Newgent was called from a distant State to preach his funeral. Truly, he was a man of God.

When the conference projected a college enterprise at Greenville, Rev. Mr. Newgent took up his residence at that place so as to give personal attention and encouragement to the institution. This college was afterwards moved to White Pine, Newgent being the leading spirit in the matter of relocation. He served as financial agent and supervised the construction of the building. Through his personal efforts the building was erected and paid for.

The evangelistic gift and executive faculty, both of which were prominent in our subject, peculiarly fitted him for the duties of Missionary Superintendent amid such conditions as the Tennessee Conference presented. Much incipient work had to be done. The routine work of his office required only a small portion of his time, leaving him free to do the work of an evangelist, to encourage weak churches and to survey new territory to conquer. This narrative has already afforded many examples of his constructive work along these lines. One more characteristic incident may not be out of place.

Near Limestone, Tennessee, was a church which was so unpromising that the quarterly conference seriously considered abandoning it and disposing of the property. It was well located, but there were strong churches on either side, and the little church, overshadowed as it was by these older organizations, had never been able to gain a proper standing.

"Let us give it another chance," said Newgent, who was presiding at the meeting. "I will hold a meeting there at the first opportunity, and we will see if it can be saved." He held the meeting accordingly and received ninety-seven members into the church, and the little, struggling church was lifted to such a position of prestige and prominence that it overshadowed its rivals, becoming a strong center of religious influence.

But it was not enough to merely get people converted and brought into the church. They must be taught in the doctrines of the church, so as not to get their doctrinal ideas from other sources.

One of the strong churches of this community was of the Dunkard order, and mainly through its influence a strong immersion sentiment prevailed. At the close of the revival there were a large number of applicants for baptism. According to prevailing custom, all expected to be immersed. It was in order on such occasions for the baptismal service to be prefaced by a sermon on baptism. Rev. Mr. Newgent took advantage of the opportunity to make some remarks on the mode of baptism, which was the one live subject in religious circles. In his discourse he said:

"We often hear people say, 'I want to be baptized as Jesus was.' I do not share this sentiment. For in one essential respect Jesus' baptism was different from ours. It was for a different purpose. He was baptized to fulfill the law; we, because we are sinners, either for the forgiveness of sins or because they are forgiven.

"But we may be baptized in the same manner in which he was baptized, and if you wish, I will tell you what that was. Paul said, 'He was made a priest like unto his brethren.' Jesus said, 'I am come, not to destroy the law or the prophets, but to fulfill.' He fulfilled every jot and tittle of the law. The law required a priest to have the water of consecration sprinkled upon his head when he was thirty years of age. Hence, if Christ was made a priest like his brethren, it is easy to see that his baptism was the same as that of the priests, his brethren, and that the water was sprinkled upon his head at the age of thirty; otherwise he would not have fulfilled every jot and tittle of the law."

A prominent Dunkard preacher present made a public statement at the close of the discourse to the effect that, while he had always believed and taught that Christ was baptized by immersion, he was now fully convinced that he had been mistaken. When they came to the baptismal service, all the applicants chose the mode of sprinkling, though they had come prepared to be immersed.

Under his capable and aggressive leadership the conference maintained a steady growth. At first its territory was confined to the eastern part of the State. But in the early nineties he, with some other ministers, advanced to the central and western parts of the State on a sort of missionary-evangelistic campaign. They held a number of meetings and were successful in winning quite a sprinkling of converts. The work thus accomplished made possible the organization of what was then known as the Tennessee River Conference in 1896.

One of the most important events in connection with the Tennessee Conference, and which was brought about mainly through his influence, occurred in 1895. It is referred to as follows in Berger's History of the United Brethren Church, page 614:

"About two years ago a movement which had been for some time in process of development, began to take definite form, resulting in considerable additions both of ministers and laymen to the United Brethren Church. The greater number of these came from the Methodist Episcopal Church, some from the M. E. Church, South, and a few from other denominations. Those coming from the Methodist churches were attracted chiefly by the milder form of episcopal government in the United Brethren Church. There was for them no possible inducement in material or worldly considerations. They could not look for larger salaries or easier fields of labor or lighter sacrifices, nor was the prospect of official promotion better than in the churches from which they came. Nor could they bring with them any of the church-houses or other property which they had aided in building. No thought or hope of this kind was entertained; much less was any effort made to do so. Influenced by principle alone, and in the face of present loss, they chose to cast in their lot with us, and they have addressed themselves earnestly to the work in their new relations. About twenty-five ministers in all, with a considerable number of members, have thus connected themselves with the United Brethren. Among the leading ministers of the movement are: Dr. T. C. Carter, Rev. W. L. Richardson, J. D. Droke, and others. They have been given a cordial welcome by the United Brethren Church, not in any spirit of proselytism, for no proselyting was done, nor from any desire to reap where others have sown, but with an open heart and door to receive any persons who love our common Lord and desire to cast their lot with us."

It seems a pity, however, that church history is so silent in regard to Rev. Mr. Newgent's connection with this event, for it was he who turned this movement toward the United Brethren Church. Those who refused to tolerate what they considered abuses of episcopal supervision in the two great Methodist bodies were in the very act of forming a new church. In this movement Dr. T. C. Carter, now Bishop Carter, occupied a conspicuous place of leadership, as he did in every great religious movement in that part of the country. His name was a household word in all that realm, and when he spoke, multitudes reverently listened. Rev. Mr. Newgent met him, and showed him a Discipline of the United Brethren Church, believing that it set forth the very principles of church government for which these great souls were contending, and thus presented the alternative of connecting themselves with a denomination that afforded what they wanted, or of adding to the number of denominational organizations which many believed were already too many. Doctor Carter suggested that Disciplines and other United Brethren literature be sent to the leading ministers of the movement. This was accordingly done; and as a result they decided to connect themselves with the United Brethren Church.

They were formally received in a special conference held in Knoxville. A number of the Bishops, general officers, and leading ministers and laymen throughout the denomination attended this conference, which was presided over by Bishop Weaver. One of the leading ministers of the movement, in delivering the welcome address on that occasion, made use of the following language:

"I am certain that one-half the membership of both churches (the Methodist bodies) heartily prefer a church government of the people, by the people, and for the people, to their own.... In view of these things, I may venture to say that a strong church that will fill the valleys and mountains of this country with a religious paper devoted to Arminianism and liberty, and will follow up this plan with men and with churches may expect a glorious welcome."

CHAPTER FOURTEEN.

Autumn—The Fading Leaf—Fruit in Old Age—His Later Labors—Present Home.

"We all do fade as a leaf," was the lamentation of an ancient prophet in a melancholy mood. The fading leaf speaks in sad but beautiful language of waning vitality. It is the harbinger of autumn, telling us that nature is getting ready to close her books for the season. It brings with it a tinge of sadness mingled with sweetness; for there is compensation in even the saddest experiences. What would the year be without the pensive days of autumn? They are the golden fringes of the bounteous summer season. Sad, indeed, would they be if the summer has been ill spent. Then might the melancholy wail arise from the forlorn heart, "The harvest is past, the summer is ended."

But when autumn looks back upon a springtime of bountiful seed-sowing, and a summer of bountiful reaping, it becomes the year's climax of joy, the beneficiary of all its blessings. Enriched by the summer's heritage, it is beautiful and peaceful and happy.

"We all do fade as a leaf." May it be said philosophically. The fading of the leaf reveals more perfectly its innate qualities, and rounds out its brief existence. The red or brown or yellow, in mute language, tells its life history and closes the book.

It is said of the aged, sometimes, "They are set in their ways." That is because in them character has become a finished product. The incidentals and accidentals have become eliminated, and the accumulated results of years of striving and hoping, sorrow and pain, defeats and victories are plainly discernible. Personal traits stand out in bold relief so that all may fittingly say, "Behold the man."

Thus, Uncle Jack—for we may now use this affectionate designation, having passed his three score and ten, is now in the autumnal glory of a life beautiful and bountiful in its fruitage. And so the autumn of his life is enriched and made fragrant by the year's benedictions. Blessed, indeed, is he to whom it is given to enjoy a long period of service, and who can then gracefully let his mantle pass to others whom God has called and prepared to receive it. To grow old sweetly, to let the sun go down amid the splendors of an unclouded evening sky, is the crowning glory of old age.

Blessed, indeed, then, is Uncle Jack. He approaches this period in life, not only in the spirit of a true philosopher, but in the spirit of a true Christian.

He still lives in the sunshine, he keeps the windows open to the breezes that bring to him the fragrance of flowers, the song of birds, and the "music of the spheres." The world smiles upon him and he returns its smile.

He has lived in an active, changing age, but has always kept up with the procession. He performed a vital part in the changing order in which he lived and moved and had his being; and he who helps to fashion events, who has a part in directing the movements of progress, is not likely to be left behind or to be trampled under foot. He not only kept pace with the world, but with a prophet's vision, he anticipated the course of human events. So, as great changes approached, he was ready to march out to meet them. Like a true prophet, he had a message for his own day and generation, but the message was more potent because he had a vision of things yet to be.

In him is illustrated the Psalmist's observation concerning the children of God, "They shall bring forth fruit in old age." For him there is no "dead line." The body may lose its agility; it may fail to do the bidding of the mind properly, but the mind and heart remain abreast of the times. The dead line means more than physical infirmity, and it often occurs that the mind lingers near that dread spot while the body is in its prime. The dead line belongs to the mind and not to the body, and hence, taking that view of it, there is no dead line for Uncle Jack.

It is given to but few men to continue in the public ministry until they pass their three score and ten. Uncle Jack had never been out of the active connection in some form from the time he entered the ministry until his seventy-third year, giving more than a half-century of unbroken service to the public work of the Church.

In the interest of accuracy and completeness, more specific mention should be made of his later work. After spending eleven years as presiding elder in Tennessee Conference, he returned North for a time, serving as pastor at Veedersburg, Indiana, as college pastor at Westfield, Illinois, as pastor at Olney, Illinois, and three years as presiding elder in Upper Wabash Conference. His work as pastor at Veedersburg included two periods, one of three years', and the other of four years' duration. This was one of the wealthiest and most influential churches in Upper Wabash Conference.

Returning to Tennessee—now East Tennessee—Conference, he was again elected to the presiding eldership, serving five years in that relation. Altogether he spent twenty-one years in the Tennessee Conference, serving five years in the pastorate besides sixteen years in the presiding elder's office.

His last work in the pastorate was at Clarinda, Iowa, being called from there to the field agency for Indiana Central University at Indianapolis by the trustees of that institution. He has always been interested in the educational work of the Church. In his varied experience in religious work he has seen demonstrated in so many ways the need of an educated ministry. So he entered upon this latter work with a deep conviction of its importance, and with the earnestness and zeal which characterized his labors all through life; but finding his physical strength insufficient for its taxing demands, he was compelled to relinquish it.

In the fall of 1910 he again attended the East Tennessee Conference session, desiring only to enjoy its fellowship. He had no thought of assuming again an active relation in the conference, but his brethren were loath to let him escape. When the election of presiding elder was called, their minds once more centered upon him, and he lacked but four votes of being the unanimous choice of the conference. This, however, brought him to face a delicate matter which set a task for his tender conscience. Seeing that his election meant the crowding of a worthy young man out of an appointment, he very generously resigned the office with instructions to the Bishop that this young man be given the place.

His present home is at Odon, Indiana. Here he finds himself among sympathetic friends, and is near the scenes of his early childhood. He takes pleasure in doing what he can in the local church, setting a wholesome example to the membership by his faithful attendance at all the services and by loyal and liberal support of all its interests. Here he enjoys the hearty good will of old and young alike, and has frequent calls for addresses at various functions, where he is always greeted with unfeigned delight.

While not employed in a regular way by the Church, an appreciative public will continue to recognize his worth, and keep ajar the door of opportunity for rendering valuable service to his fellow men.

CHAPTER FIFTEEN.

Character Sketch.

The analysis of a flower is the work, not of the florist, but of the botanist. The florist sees in the combination of the various parts the beauty of a perfected whole, while the botanist sees the parts separated and classified but loses sight of the flower itself. The florist's viewpoint is preferable to that of the botanist. This is no less true in dealing with human life than in the treatment of a flower. However, in the interest of thoroughness, some attention should be given to a study of the particular elements of character which give to our subject his peculiar individuality and made possible that degree of eminence which he has won for himself. The task is not an easy one. This is true in the case of all men of superior strength. The sources of power are so embedded in the depths of one's personality as to make them difficult to trace. In the presence of such men we are instinctively aware of their superiority, but if asked to give a reason for our impressions we would be unable to do so. The power of a personality is to be felt rather than explained or analyzed. It is this invisible, undefinable something that lifts the man above the level of the commonplace and gives him a commanding influence among his fellows.

The strength of some characters is due to one or two exceptionally strong traits, while in other particulars they may be correspondingly weak. The world sees only the mountain peaks of strength and upon them it builds its estimate of the man. To this rule Rev. A. J. Newgent is one of the rare exceptions. "Like a tree planted by the rivers of water," the distinctive feature of his life is rather in the full and symmetrical development of the various qualities of mature and well-rounded manhood. Hence, he is essentially a man of the people—not a man of one class, but of all classes, the embodiment of the true spirit of democracy. Like Paul, he can be all things to all men without sacrificing principle or dignity or losing the respect of any of them. His sympathies are broad and deep, and go out to all alike. There is no assumed or conscious superiority to create a barrier between himself and the humblest soul. He observes no arbitrary distinctions. Whoever he chances to meet is at once a friend and brother. He possesses in a large degree the rare faculty of making people feel at home in his presence. Fads and snobs and artificiality he hates as he hates sin. The glitter and tinsel show of life are counted as dross, but the pure gold of human character that needs no outward adornment is his delight.

His well-balanced temperament enables him to so adjust himself to different conditions, that he is invariably master of the situation in which he may be placed. In the home, whether marked by riches or poverty, culture or illiteracy, he is always the same genial guest. To the children, young people, and old folks alike, the presence of "Uncle Jack" is always welcome. In his public ministry, whatever the demands of the occasion, he is ready to meet them. Never is he at the mercy of his surroundings. Not many months ago, while doing service as field secretary for Indiana Central University, he was secured by the pastor of a country church to hold an all-day meeting. The morning program was interfered with by a severe rainstorm, so that besides himself and the pastor, only three persons were present. Yet, he preached to his small audience with his wonted zeal and earnestness, the effort being pronounced by those who heard it superior to the one in the afternoon, when he had the inspiration of a full house.

He never follows the beaten paths simply because others have walked therein. The fact that some one else did a thing in a certain way is not sufficient reason why he should proceed upon the same plan. He imitates no one and it is safe to say no one imitates him, for the reason that he is so intensely original; the processes of his mind are so completely his own that no one could well repeat them. Bishop Edwards once said, "There is one man whose sermons no one has ever tried to copy; that man is Newgent." This originality has been a valuable asset in debate. His opponent might come with his mind well furnished with all the laws of logic, the tactics known to debaters, and the arguments on both sides of the question well in hand, only to find his materials practically useless. Rev. Mr. Newgent's method being so unique, his approach to the subject from such unexpected angles, and his presentation of unheard-of arguments in defending his position, while transgressing no valid law of debate or of logic, made him a law unto himself. The opinions of other men rather than being accepted as authority, only serve to quicken his thought and incite to investigation. In preaching he is purely extemporaneous, often deferring the selection of a text or theme until after he enters the pulpit. But his resourceful mind, well stocked with information, the result of general reading and observation, and his aptness at illustration, rendered safe for him what to some men would be a hazardous undertaking.

While original in his thinking, he never discredits the opinions of others, no matter how widely they may differ from his own. Honesty and sincerity he regards as superior to articles of faith. "If no one gets to heaven except those who believe as I do," he often says, "the audience there will be rather small." David said, in his haste, "All men are liars." If Rev. Mr. Newgent should err in his judgment of mankind, it would more likely be in the opposite direction. A source of strength is his faith in men, their possibilities and aspirations for better things. To be a leader of men, this faith is imperative. Beneath the surface shale of human differences, selfishness and error, may be found a sub-stratum of genuine manhood. And upon this the true builder must build. He must recognize that he is dealing with intelligent beings who can think and feel, and who are possessed with a sense of honor and self-respect. The man who would inspire others to higher things must not despise or ignore these vital factors of individual consciousness. There are sacred precincts in every life which the owner has a right to guard as with a flaming sword, and which should not be approached except with unsandaled feet and sanctified hands. That there is more real incentive to noble effort in a vision of the possibilities and beauty of a noble life than in the lash, is a prominent article in Rev. Mr. Newgent's faith. The spirit of "anti-ism" and the methods used by a certain type of evangelists of pouring out the vials of their sarcastic and vituperative wrath upon men and things in general are offensive to him in the extreme. Hence, the positive note is always dominant in his preaching.

The secret of getting on with men is in knowing what chord to strike to get the desired response. That he knows well the secret, the achievements of his career bear ample testimony. An incident in his boyhood may not be out of place here, as it illustrates the principle by which he has been actuated throughout his entire life in his relations with men. He was employed at a saw-mill. The logs were hauled from the forest to the mill with oxen. That an ox team is no friend to grace, is the general verdict of those who have experimental knowledge of ox-driving. One large, burly team in particular that was noted for obstinacy and general degeneracy, had defied all the skill and whips and profanity the driver could produce. He repeatedly had gone to the woods for his load and returned with the empty wagon. At a critical point in the road the team would balk and refuse to budge until the wagon was unloaded. It became a standing challenge to the entire crowd, different ones of whom accepted the challenge, with the same result. Finally Jack, as he was then called, asked permission to try. He was only a spindling lad of a hundred-weight avoirdupois, and the very suggestion was met with jeers. "Have you ever driven oxen?" he was asked. "No," was the reply, "but I think I have ox sense." They finally consented, but no one expected anything but another failure. The driver offered him the whip. "I don't need the whip," he said, and started for his charge. He made friends with his dumb servants, rubbed their ears, spoke to them coaxingly, and soon had them on the way to the woods. He took the precaution to provide himself with a small bag of corn. He succeeded in getting the log on the wagon and again patted the oxen, and as a reward of merit, gave them each a nubbin, letting them see that there was more in the bag that would be available if they proved worthy. Thus, as he said, he "sooked" them along, and to the astonishment of the mill hands, arrived in an unusually short time with a large log. It was not only a lesson to the men, but to himself as well, by which he has profited throughout his entire life. He has verified the fact many times that "sooking" will succeed with men as well as oxen when the whip will fail.

There are two kinds of leadership among men. One is the arbitrary leadership of the boss; the other is natural, a true leadership, which has for its basis personal strength and merit. The former is transient, having no real place among thinking and liberty-loving people. The other is abiding, for the true leader is ever in demand.

This latter type is quaintly set forth in Longfellow's "Song of Hiawatha":

"As unto the bow the cord is,

So is unto man the woman;

While she bends him, she obeys him,

Though she leads him, yet she follows."

It is the woman's leadership—controlling by obedience, leading by following. A paradox, perhaps, but supported by the logic of actual achievements in every realm of human endeavor. The workman controls the force of a stream by obeying that force. Should he plant his turbine on the hilltop and command the water to flow up the hill and turn the wheel, the stream would only laugh at his impudence as it rippled on its way. But when he plants his wheel in the current, the stream at once becomes his servant. It is the principle observed by the engineer, the sailor, the electrician, or the aviator in harnessing and utilizing the various forces of nature. The same principle lies at the basis of all true leadership in society, church, or state. The strict observance of it has enabled Rev. Mr. Newgent to touch the motive springs of character by means of which men are aroused to action. His close sympathy with men ever gives him an unconscious, commanding influence. And this influence is always turned to account in their own uplifting and in the advancement of righteousness. Out of over a half-century in the public ministry, about one-half of his time has been spent as presiding elder. This official relation does not afford the opportunity for evangelistic and other forms of direct church work as does the pastorate; so that definite, visible results cannot readily be computed. Yet, few men have built for themselves greater or more enduring monuments in the line of tangible results. More than six thousand members have been gathered into the denomination through his labors. Thirty church-houses stand to his credit as a church builder. He has officiated at about one hundred dedicatory exercises, a recognition of his ability as a money-getter. On Chautauqua platforms and special occasions of both a religious and semi-religious character he has been a prominent figure. And his advice is always at a premium in the counsels of the denomination.

It has been well said, "When God made wit, he pronounced it good." Rev. Mr. Newgent has demonstrated the practical utility of sanctified wit and humor. It is possible, however, that his humor has led to more misconception of his character than any other thing that could be mentioned. The trait that touches the most popular chord is likely to be so magnified as to shut from view others of equal or greater significance. The fame of an author not infrequently rests upon a single production, and that by no means his best. Edward Eggleston did not regard the "Hoosier Schoolmaster" as the best of his works, but multitudes who have been charmed by that simple story will never know that he ever wrote anything else.

That Rev. Mr. Newgent has in some degree suffered in a similar manner is, therefore, nothing more than might be expected. Yet, if his humor, in the minds of some, would reduce him to the level of a mere jokesmith, to him it has been an invaluable asset. It has served to open the way for the assertion of the more substantial and practical qualities; it has enabled him to capture hostile and even riotous audiences; with it he has battered down strongholds of opposition; it has been an effective weapon against false doctrine, hypocrisy, and deep-seated vice in its various forms; it has served as the sugar coating for truths that were unpleasant because of a perverted taste; he has found it a splendid tonic to dispense with more solid food to aid the digestion of mental and spiritual dyspeptics. His humor is of the spontaneous sort, ready to boil over whenever the lid is removed. It flows out through his discourses and conversations as naturally as the stream gushes from the fountain, and is always mellowed by tenderness and a deep human sympathy.

"Where dwellest thou?" was asked of the Son of Man. The question was of greater significance than the interrogator supposed, and the answer was even more significant. The Savior did not say, in Galilee or Palestine, or Nazareth, but simply, "Come and see." A man's habitation is not a matter of geographical boundary. Should the question be addressed to Rev. Mr. Newgent, he would say, "I live on the sunny side of the street." A critic of Emerson said that because of his unorthodoxy he was doomed to go to hell. A contemporary who was acquainted with Emerson's kindly and genial disposition remarked that if he did, he would change the climate. Rev. Mr. Newgent not only lives on the sunny side of the street, but he carries sunshine with him. He has a knack of distilling sunshine from every circumstance of life. He changes the climate to suit his own temperament. With Solomon, he believes in the medical virtues of a smile, that "a merry heart doeth good like a medicine."

He was once called to visit a woman in the mountains of east Tennessee, whom he had never seen. She was supposed to be dying of consumption. It was late at night when he arrived and the weather was inclement. The physician was leaving the house as he approached. On learning who he was, the physician told him he was too late; the lady was dying. He went at once to her bedside, and found that the death sweat had begun to gather and the death rattle was in her throat. He lifted up her head gently and spoke to her. Her face brightened, and presently she began to talk. She told him that she was glad he had come, that she must soon die, and feared she would have to go without seeing him.

But in a voice tender but cheerful, he told her he was glad to do her any favor, and added, "But don't be in a hurry about going. I wouldn't go to-night, if I were you. The night is dark and stormy, and you might get lost in these mountains. You had better wait until morning. It will be so much better to go in the day time." She smiled at the eccentricity of the remarks, and seemed to make up her mind to take the advice. Morning found her much improved, having apparently decided to postpone the matter indefinitely. And contrary to the predictions of her physician and friends, she recovered to thank the preacher rather than the physician for prolonging her days.

To him there are "sermons in stone, and books in the running brooks." He finds in the commonest things and most commonplace occurrence of everyday life, lessons of practical truth that enrich and adorn his discourses. Once while in his company we were stopping at a hotel for dinner. While we were seated at the table, some one dropped a coin in the slot of an automatic music machine, at which it began to grind out a familiar tune. Rev. Mr. Newgent on observing the operation, quoted the language of Job, "I caused the widow's heart to sing for joy," and added, "Don't you suppose that was Job's way of making people sing for joy—with a bit of money?" And subsequently the illustration was used with fine effect in a discourse on benevolence.

Underlying all, and harmonizing all the elements of his personality is a firm and abiding faith in God. It is doubtless easier for some persons to be religious than for others. In this respect he has been favored. The natural bent of his mind from earliest childhood was toward religion. Converted at the age of ten, his entire life has been controlled by a strong and steady devotion to religious ideals. His faith is broad and well balanced. Religious affectation and fads have no part with him. His religious character was formed amid the strife and controversies of various creeds in a day when creed was everything. These controversies drove him to a critical study of the various systems of theology in the light of the Bible. He made the Word of God his sole authority in all doctrinal matters. That which he recognized as supported by the Book, he made his own. That he defended without apology or compromise. While he is dogmatic to a large degree, his dogmatism is of a practical sort. He believes that there is a vital relation between doctrine and Christian character. A true life cannot be built upon erroneous or crooked theology. He often deplores the fact that the church has swung away from the strict, doctrinal teaching of the past, believing that in consequence it has suffered the loss of spiritual vitality and zeal.

His faith is as simple as it is broad and deep. The essentials of religion are few and easily comprehended. The simplicity of gospel truth when properly presented is one of its strongest attractive elements. In many instances the simple gospel has been complicated and obscured by a mass of theological rubbish heaped up by men more interested in a creed than in the ultimate truth. If the rubbish is cleared away, the truth will shine forth clear and distinct in its beauty, and men will accept it. To remove the rubbish and give a clear setting to the simple, vital elements of Christian faith seems to have been a large part of his appointed task. This is among his chief contributions to the cause of pure and undefiled religion.

To the simplicity of his faith should be added another quality, perhaps best described by the word "practical." With him faith is an intensely practical thing. The faith that expresses itself merely in stock phrases, articles of a creed or church membership is, to say the least, a base counterfeit, a useless commodity. Nothing seems to him more irreligious than the religion that begins and ends in noise. Genuine faith has a personal, spiritual, and commercial value. Its highest expression is in doing something that ought to be done. It crystallizes into character, and contributes to human welfare. It places its possessor upon the broad highway of the world's need, bringing him into sympathetic touch with the throbbing heart-life of humanity. Thus he maintains the sound Scriptural philosophy that faith is to be tested by works.

The church has profited largely from his beneficence. A habit which he has followed throughout his ministry is, as he says, "to live like a poor man and give like a rich man"—that is, like a rich man ought to give. He never turns down a worthy call for help. Even should there be a question as to the merit of the call, he usually gives it the benefit of the doubt. "His house is known to all the vagrant train," and, to borrow another quaint phrase from Goldsmith, "even his faults lean to virtue's side." The tramp that comes to his door gets with his dinner a genial smile and wholesome words of admonition, even though the dinner, the smile, and the admonition are lost upon a worthless subject.

In dedicating churches he has made it a general rule to give his own subscription for an amount equal to the largest on the list. On a number of occasions, under pressure of a great need, he has pledged more than he was worth, in the faith that God would open the way for meeting the obligation. And his faith in every such case has been vindicated. His life illustrates the Bible doctrine of increasing by scattering. He surely has scattered with a lavish hand. He has not only observed the Lord's tithe in his benevolence, but has gone quite beyond it, even to the giving, in some instances, of the greater part of his income to the Lord's cause. Yet with it all, he has increased in temporal possessions. He has honored God with his substance, and God has smiled graciously upon him, so that with David he can well say, "I once was young, but now am old, yet have I not seen the righteous forsaken, nor his seed begging bread."

CHAPTER SIXTEEN.

"Lights Out"—A Dirge of the War.

A marked characteristic of Uncle Jack, as these pages have shown, is his peculiar ability to establish and maintain strong ties of personal friendship. This has been evident even from his youth. He has gathered friends from all walks of life, and their name is legion. The list has always been characterized by names that were written large in the annals of Church and State. Conspicuous among these is the late Lieutenant-Colonel James T. Johnson, of Rockville, Indiana, a man distinguished for talent and achievement in various fields. The twain were boys together, and the friendship thus early formed continued until severed by the death of Johnston in 1904. When Newgent was first winning laurels as a boy preacher, Johnston often walked five miles to attend his services. They were young men, mere youths, when the Civil War broke out. Both heard and responded to their country's call at that dark time when not only the country's honor, but her very existence was at stake. Both served under General Burnsides, and both held official positions in the army, Newgent as chaplain of his regiment, and Johnston as lieutenant, later lieutenant-colonel. After the war was over, each won honors and served well his generation in his chosen profession, the one as a minister of the gospel, the other as a lawyer and politician. Johnston found room near the top in the legal profession, and at the same time represented his district three successive terms in Congress. He ranked high as an orator, and, like his clerical friend, was much in demand at reunions and other gatherings of the soldiers, the two men frequently dividing time upon such occasions. Had Newgent chosen politics as a career, he would doubtless have become a political leader. Had Johnston turned his attention to the ministry, he would have taken rank in all probability among the leading preachers of his day.

But there was one sad difference between them—Johnston was skeptically inclined. While the two men maintained the highest regard for each other, and frequently were associated together in their work, the subject of religion was one point on which, to the regret, possibly, of both parties, they were not in accord. Johnston's skepticism however, was not of the positive sort. He represented the honest doubter rather than the avowed disbeliever. His wife was a devout Presbyterian, and while he could not subscribe to the tenets of the church, he never disparaged the church or its work. Every worthy cause found in him a sympathizer and liberal supporter. His honor and integrity were never questioned, and he enjoyed the full confidence and esteem of his fellows. It is a matter of satisfaction that such a life was not permitted to go out in the dark. And Newgent had the joy of finally leading him, just as his sun was sinking below the horizon, to a simple faith in Christ and a blessed assurance of his acceptance with God.

During his last illness, which covered a period of six months, the colonel was visited frequently by local ministers, but owing to his reputed skepticism and his high professional standing, the subject of religion was not pressed upon him. There is a tendency to fear big men in matters of religion not easily explained and not easily overcome, and it is quite probable that many a great life has ended without the consolations of religion that, were it not for this tendency, might have been led into the light as readily as a little child. Oh, how Christians fear the logic of the world, and yet, the sword of the Spirit is a greater weapon than all the world's artillery!

Newgent visited him almost daily during this time, and on one occasion determined to broach the subject of religion. "Colonel," he said, in his usual tactful manner, "while you are shut in here, would it not be a fine opportunity for you to read the Bible through?"

"Well," he answered, "Laura and I tried it; we took it up by books, but we got stalled." It was, of course, the colonel himself who "got stalled." Laura, his wife, was a Christian, as has been noted, and her faith was not shaken by Scriptural difficulties.

"What was your trouble?" Newgent questioned, with a view to encouraging conversation along that channel.

"Well," he said, "we got to the book of Job. I could not reconcile the book of Job with the idea that God is our Heavenly Father, full of love and mercy. If Job was God's child and a good man, as the Bible says he was, how could a loving father allow a loving, obedient child to be so abused and tempted by the devil? I can't see through it."

After he had delivered his speech on the difficulties of the book of Job, and unburdened his mind somewhat, Newgent drew near to him, and speaking very simply but earnestly, said: "Colonel, you are a great lawyer, but you are only a child in the Bible. Your trouble is that you commenced at the wrong place. When, as a little child, you started to school, your teacher did not start you in the advanced studies. She put you in the A, B, C class. Now, don't be in too big a hurry to get out of your A, B, C's in the study of the Bible, for there is where you belong. I have been making a study of God's Word for many years, and I want you to listen to me a while. I think we can get over the rough places after a while. Do you have any trouble with Jesus Christ? He was God's dear son, yet he had to suffer more than any man, but his suffering was for others. So we learn from Job's sufferings that he has helped millions to trust God in the dark."

This was the colonel's A, B, C lesson in religion. The visits and conversations were continued day after day, until a couple of days before his death, when the truths of the preceding lessons were clinched in the following conversation:

"Colonel," said the preacher, resuming their lessons, "you had one of the best mothers in the world, did you not?" He admitted that he had.

"She taught you to say your little prayers?"

"Yes," said the great man, as the tears started from his eyes.

"And you never doubted her word?"

"No—never."

"That was simple faith in mother. Now, in your mind go back to mother, and though she is dead, look up into her face as when you were a child, and trust her as you did then. That will represent the soul looking up to Jesus and trusting him for salvation. That is all Christ requires of a sinner."

As the preacher finished this little homily on faith, the colonel was weeping like a child. "Jack," he sobbed, "is that all there is in coming to Christ to be saved?"

"That is all there is," and before the preacher could continue the discussion further, the light broke in upon the humble and contrite heart. "I've got it," he interrupted with much emotion, at the same time grasping the preacher's hand with all the strength his six-months' illness had left him. Thus, the man who all the years of his eventful career, by his own wisdom and logic and learning knew not God, was at the last critical moment melted and transformed by the light from Calvary, and a great life was snatched as a brand from the eternal burning. The lawyer, the statesman, the scholar, the orator received the kingdom of heaven on the Savior's easy terms, "as a little child," and two days later his soul passed into the presence of Jehovah.

Rev. Mr. Newgent delivered the funeral oration. Men of prominence from various parts of the country helped to swell the vast throng that was present at the funeral service. The story of the colonel's conversion from skepticism to simple, saving faith in Christ was related by the speaker, and produced a profound impression.

The paper with which this chapter is concluded refers to the life-long association of the two men, Johnston, the "young cavalryman of Indiana," and Newgent, the "boy chaplain." It was read before a special meeting of the Steele Post G. A. R., and auxiliary orders of Rockville shortly after Johnston's death by Mrs. White, the wife of Judge A. F. White of that city. Judge White was also a soldier and a life-long friend of Johnston and Newgent. The doctor referred to in the paper had served as a physician in the Confederate army, but afterward took up his residence in Rockville, where he built up a large practice. The three men were present with the wife when Colonel Johnston died, and helped to make up the scene in the death chamber so dramatically described in the paper.

"LIGHTS OUT."

"It is midwinter in east Tennessee in 1863. The rivers are flooded, the valleys desolate, the mountain gaps gorged with snow. It is the home of mountain patriots; it must be held at all hazards to the last. This is Lincoln's solemn wish; it is a part of Grant's giant plan when Mission Ridge is stormed. A young cavalryman of Indiana is one of the ten thousand who keep freedom's vigils along the Clinch, the Holstein, and the French Broad. He munches his meager rations of parched corn; he rides the wild mountain roads night and day; he obeys to the letter his orders to hold to the last man the ford of a remote mountain stream. A buckshot buries itself in his wrist, making a wound which heals long after the war and a scar which he carries to his grave. The old flag stays in east Tennessee.

"He has a comrade from a neighboring county who shares with him the suffering and sacrifice of that desperate campaign, he is the "boy chaplain" of the brigade.

"It is the same winter along the Rappahannock and the Rappidan. The snow, like a measureless shroud, covers the numberless dead of the debatable land between the Potomac and the James. There is another soldier, a mere boy, a young artilleryman from the Shenandoah, who is one of the thousands who hold Lee's unbroken lines. His battery long since won its title to glory. It helped to clear the mountain gaps of the Blue Ridge; its red guns helped feed the fires which lighted up the valley of death for Pickett's dauntless charge. Ill fed, ragged, but inbred with the chivalry of the South, he is in it all. There is victory at Chancellorsville, but defeat at Gettysburg; but St. Andrew's cross still gleams blood red on the breast of the South, The Stars and Bars still flash defiance from Marye's Hill.

"The young artilleryman also has a comrade from the valley, a young trooper who rides with Ashby's cavaliers in all their wild forays.

"Two flags, two oaths of allegiance, the culminating hates of a hundred years, separate these two young soldiers of the North and the South. But they are not alien in blood, they are brothers of the same race, Anglo-Saxon from the first Americans to the last. They speak the same tongue, their mothers read the same Bible, prayed to the same God; their forefathers fought for the same country—Nathaniel Greene at Yorktown, Washington on Cambridge Heights.

"It is midsummer of 1904. The cavalryman of '63 is dying; not in the weary hospital of pain; not on the perilous edge of battle. More than forty years have passed since the grim midwinter of east Tennessee.

"It is the home he has made for his declining years. The rooms are cool and sweet, a broad porch looks down a quiet street, familiar books are everywhere; his escutcheon over the mantel shows his soldier record from '62 to '65—the old, old story of duty and glory. A blue book on the table tells briefly his struggle from the farm to the halls of Congress; the faces of statesmen, kinsmen, and friends look down from their appropriate places on the walls.

"The good right hand of the veteran lies in that of another; grief-stricken she keeps her vows, 'till death do us part.'

"A grey-haired man holds the other. It is the soldier of the Rappahannock. Lee's battery boy of '63 is the trusted physician, the medical confidant, and ministrant of the Union soldier. With all the knowledge of a learned and skillful physician, he has fought the common enemy for the life of his dying friend. But the odds are too great. Old pains, old ailments, old wounds of '63 outmatch the medical arts of 1904. But the doctor has known the grief of defeat before. Once a long time ago he yielded to the inevitable in the orchards of Appomattox. He lays his ear close over the failing heart to catch, if he can, its last lingering drum-beats in the battle of life. He places his fingers on the pulseless wrist, searching for its last faint throb—and they rest motionless for a moment on the old scar of '63. 'It is over,' he says very softly.

"A low word of prayer for the widow and fatherless falls from the lips of the grey-haired minister at the foot of the bed. It is the 'boy chaplain' of the dead veteran's old brigade—youthful to the end. Another man beside him, thin-visaged and bent. It is Ashby's old trooper, and his eyes are full of tears as he walks slowly out of the room.

"'Lights out.' 'The bands in the pine woods cease. A robin sings close by, as they will in summer evenings; the fragrance of old-fashioned flowers steals in through the white window curtains. The sun sinks behind the church across the street, the shadow of its belfry coming in at the open door. And over all, Lincoln's worn face looks down from its place among the pictures on the wall. Even now with the hush of death upon us all, we hear his plaintive prophecy of long ago: 'We are not enemies but friends. We must not be enemies. Though passion may have strained, it cannot break the bonds of our affection. The mystic chord of memory, stretching from every patriot grave and battlefield to every living heart and hearthstone all over this broad land, will yet swell the chorus of the Union when touched again, as they surely will be, by the better angels of our nature.'"